Spanish
B I B L E

C
&

Spanish
BIBLE

Margaret Barca

Contents

Introduction   1

Spanish Basics   3

Tapas   11

Soups & Stews   61

Seafood   85

Vegetable Dishes & Salads   113

Paellas &
Other Plates to Share   147

Sweets   193

Extras   237

Special Ingredients   248

Conversions   250

Index   252

Introduction

Fresh, simple, regional, seasonal – these qualities are at the heart of classic Spanish food. While 'new wave' Spanish cooking is often startlingly inventive, for most day-to-day meals traditional dishes still prevail. Vegetables, eggs, olive oil, fresh and cured meats – including the paprika-spiked sausage chorizo, the country's renowned ham (jamon) and salted cod (*bacalao*) – are just some of the time-honoured produce that is central to Spain's varied cuisines.

The Spanish love their food and they love sharing it – be it the snack-sized morsels known as tapas, or larger dishes such as paella, perfect for special occasions. Variety and flexibility are key: you can size up tapas to make a meal or divide larger dishes to serve as snacks. The Spanish appetite isn't about size – it's about the love of good food, and of authentic flavours derived from local produce and regional traditions.

This book provides an easy-to-follow introduction to the classic flavours that are intrinsic to Spain's cuisine.

Spanish Basics

The cuisine of Spain is rich with heritage, acknowledging influences from the Arab world and the Americas; as well as traditional peasant life, the bounty of the surrounding seas, the relatively equable Mediterranean climate, and the harsher conditions and landscape of some inland regions. In the north, French customs emerge in the hearty, long-braised dishes of beans and cured sausage. Further south, in Andalusia in particular, the use of saffron and other spices, figs, oranges and nuts are a tangible reminder of Moorish influences.

Ingredients

A few distinctive ingredients permeate typically Spanish cuisine. Including some of these in your cooking will help capture the true flavours of Spain.

All varieties of **anchovies** are widely used in Spanish cooking. The most familiar are the pinkish-brown variety, which are salt-cured and then canned or bottled in oil. A Mediterranean specialty, increasingly available in Australia and the US, are 'white' anchovies, known as *boquerones*. These are simply filleted anchovies marinated in vinegar, which gives them a softer texture and a more subtle flavour.

Dried **salt cod** (*bacalao*) looks unpromising: large, slightly curled slabs of pale dried fish usually encrusted with salt. But once it has been soaked and cooked, you will understand why it is such a favourite ingredient in Spanish cooking. To prepare, rinse well, place in a bowl, cover with cold water and leave in the refrigerator for 48 hours. (Change the water twice a day to remove excess salt and rehydrate the fish.) Drain, and rinse again. It is now ready to be cooked.

Meats such as the spicy, sometimes fiery, **chorizo** sausage and **jamon** (pronounced 'ha-*mon*'), a dry-cured ham cut in wafer-thin slices, are other much used ingredients. Jamon comes in different grades but all are delicious: jamon Iberico is one of Spain's most famous exports, however jamon serrano is less expensive and is a fine substitute. If you can't find jamon, use Italian prosciutto, or a smoked ham, instead.

Morcilla, the Spanish version of blood sausage or black pudding, consists of pigs' blood, onion and rice, with spices (notably *pimenton*). It is frequently served as tapa, thickly sliced and lightly fried; it is also a frequent addition to soups and stews.

Spanish wine has been enjoying a rise in international recognition and popularity, and none more so than **sherry** – or *Jerez* – named after the town where this forti-fied wine has been produced for many centuries. Sherry can range from the very pale, dry, *fino* sherries, to the darker, sweeter (and higher in alcohol) *oloroso* styles. One of the most sought-after sherries is **Pedro Ximenez**, some-times known just as PX – a dark, luscious sweet sherry made from the sun-dried Pedro Ximenez grape variety. Use PX to enrich slow-cooked meat dishes, or as the per-fect complement to creamy Spanish desserts and cakes.

Spain is renowned for its **olive oil**. More than 200 olive varieties are grown and the country is the world's larg-est exporter of olive oil. Like all Mediterranean nations, the Spanish use olive oil liberally in their cooking. It is common to drizzle a little (or a lot!) onto any savoury dish, and it is baked into cakes and biscuits and, of course, used extensively for frying. Rich and fruity extra-virgin olive oil is especially good for eating with bread, salads, vegetables and soups.

Various small, mild **pimientos** (chilli peppers) are used – both fresh and preserved – in many Spanish dishes. Popular varieties include **piquillo** and **padron** and they are added to salads and tortillas, stuffed with tuna or salted cod, or roasted over coals, drizzled with oil and offered as simple tapas.

Spanish paprika (*pimenton*) is a staple ingredient in Spanish cooking. Made from red pimientos which have been smoked and ground, Spanish paprika is available in sweet (*dulce*), mild (*agridulce*) and hot (*picante*) varieties. Spanish paprika is quite different to the Hungarian style more commonly available in Australia and the US, due to its distinctive smoky flavour. You can substitute smoked paprika, if the Spanish variety can't be found.

The Moors brought **saffron** to Spain more than a thousand years ago and today, Spain is the world's largest producer of the spice. Saffron's subtle fragrance and vibrant colour is integral to many Spanish dishes – particularly seafood – and gives paella its rich golden hue.

Aromatic, with complex flavours, true Spanish **sherry vinegar** (*Vinagre de Jerez*) – made from sherry produced in the Jerez region of southern Spain – adds a distinctive taste to dressings, sauces and soups.

Spaniards love shellfish. Scrub **mussel** and **clam** shells and rinse under cold running water. To debeard mussels, pull off the tuft of bristly hairs at the junction of the shells. Tap any shells that are slightly open; if they don't close immediately, discard. After cooking, discard any shells that do not open up.

Freshly caught **octopus** can be tough and rubbery, and requires tenderising before being cooked. Check with your fishmonger – often octopus sold retail has already been tenderised. To prepare the octopus, use a sharp knife to cut the head from the tentacles below the hard beak. Push the beak up and out, then discard. Turn the body inside-out and remove all internal organs and the ink sac. Use the knife to slice away the eye. Rinse well.

The Spanish often keep the tails when cooking **prawns**, so check the recipe before following these instructions. Remove the legs and head, and then peel off the shell, including the tail. Use a sharp knife to make an incision along the back and remove the digestive tract.

Squid and **calamari** are widely used in Spanish cooking. The smaller they are the more tender. To prepare, put into a sink of cold water and rinse well. Pull the tentacles away from the hood tube (the innards should come with them), cut to sever. Rinse tentacles and set aside. Grasp the transparent spine inside the hood and pull it out. Rinse the hood until clean, then peel off the thin, coloured layer of skin and discard.

There is more information on Spanish ingredients on page 248.

Equipment

While you don't need any special dishes to cook Spanish food, you may decide to invest in these for an authentic effect.

Cazuela – glazed terracotta dish which comes in various shapes and sizes, used for both cooking and serving Spanish food. They are fired to a very high density and retain heat well. Cazuelas are available from many cookware stores.When using a cazuela over direct heat, it is best to use a heat diffuser.

Paellera (often simply called a paella pan) – a large, round, shallow pan, (traditionally cast-iron with two handles), designed for cooking and serving paella. The width allows more surface area for the crisp crust (*socarrat*) which should develop on the bottom of good paella. If you can't find a paellera, a large, not-too-heavy (this helps the rice cook evenly) frying pan will do instead.

Tapas

As one version of the story goes, a *tapa* (the word literally means 'cover' or 'lid') was a piece of bread placed over a glass of wine by workers in the field to keep insects away. Later, it became the custom to add some ham or cheese to the bread, to be served as a snack with a drink.

Today tapas can be anything from a simple bowl of olives, spicy little empanadas stuffed with tuna, to a *cazuela* of sizzling prawns; heady with the fragrance of garlic. These morsels are the perfect accompaniment to a chilled sherry, a Spanish beer or light red wine. Or you can serve several tapas as a starter, or larger quantities (*raciones*) together to make a meal.

< Artichoke & Jamon Empanadas (page 12)

Artichoke & Jamon Empanadas

Serves 4

150 g (5 oz) marinated artichokes, drained and roughly chopped

60 g (2 oz) jamon (or prosciutto), chopped

120 g (4 oz) Swiss cheese, grated

1 egg, separated, yolks lightly beaten

freshly ground black pepper

250 g (9 oz) ready-rolled puff pastry

Preheat the oven to 220°C (420°F). Line two baking trays with baking paper.

Mix artichokes in a small bowl with jamon, cheese and egg yolk. Season with pepper.

Cut the pastry into 8-cm (2½-in) circles. Spoon a little of the artichoke mixture into the centre of each pastry round, fold over to form a semicircle and pinch pastry together to seal. Place on the prepared baking trays.

Brush empanadas with egg white. Place in preheated oven and bake for 20 minutes. Serve hot.

Anchovy & Egg Toast

Tostados

Makes 12 pieces

12 thick slices breadstick

2 cloves garlic, halved

3 eggs

2 tablespoons (40 ml/1½ fl oz) milk

salt and freshly ground black pepper

2 tablespoons (40 ml/1⅓ fl oz) extra-virgin olive oil

6–8 anchovies in oil, well drained and chopped

2 tablespoons baby capers, drained

Toast the bread until just golden. Rub cut garlic over toasted bread.

Lightly whisk the eggs with the milk and season with salt and pepper.

Heat 1 tablespoon of the oil in a non-stick pan over low heat. Add egg mixture and cook, stirring, until almost scrambled but still creamy. Stir in the anchovy pieces.

Pile scrambled egg onto the garlic toasts, drizzle with a little oil and scatter with capers. Serve immediately.

Asparagus with Scrambled Eggs

Serves 4

8 spears young asparagus,
   tough ends trimmed

4 large eggs

1 teaspoon sweet or hot
   Spanish paprika

pinch of salt

3 tablespoons (60 ml/2 fl oz)
   olive oil

1 clove garlic, thinly sliced

Place asparagus in boiling water and blanch for a few minutes, until it starts to soften but is still bright green. Strain and cut into pieces about 2.5 cm (1 in) long.

Beat the eggs in a bowl with paprika and salt.

Heat the oil in a non-stick frying pan over medium heat. Add garlic and fry for 1 minute, then add asparagus pieces and sauté for a further minute. Add beaten eggs to the pan and cook over low heat, stirring all the time, until eggs are almost set.

Remove from heat (they will continue to cook, but should stay creamy) and serve immediately.

✕ You can serve this tapa in small bowls or piled onto toast. Choose small young asparagus spears (traditionally wild asparagus is used).

Broad Beans with Jamon

Serves 4–6

1 tablespoon (20 ml/¾ fl oz) olive oil

1 clove garlic, crushed

½ red onion, finely chopped

180 g (6½ oz) jamon (or prosciutto), roughly chopped

2 tablespoons (40 ml/1½ fl oz) dry sherry

3 cups shelled broad beans, fresh or frozen

½ cup (125 ml/4 fl oz) chicken or vegetable stock

salt and freshly ground black pepper

Heat the oil in a non-stick frying pan over medium heat. Add garlic and onion, and sauté for 3–4 minutes until softened. Add jamon and sauté for another 3–4 minutes. Pour sherry into pan and cook until absorbed. Add the broad beans and stock, stirring to combine, and bring to boil. Reduce the heat, cover, and simmer for about 10 minutes.

Check seasoning and add pepper if needed. Serve warm or at room temperature.

✕ Add some sliced hard-boiled eggs and serve with crusty bread for a light lunch.

Baked Garlic Mushroom Caps

Serves 4–6

60 g (2 oz) butter, melted

2 tablespoons (40 ml/1½ fl oz) olive oil

1 cup fresh breadcrumbs

½ cup chopped garlic chives

salt and freshly ground black pepper

1 kg (2 lb 3 oz) button mushrooms, stems removed

Preheat oven to 180°C (360°F).

Mix butter, oil, breadcrumbs and chives in a bowl, and season with salt and pepper, to taste.

Spoon the breadcrumb mix into the mushroom caps, pressing it down well. Place mushrooms on a non-stick baking tray, put in preheated oven and bake for about 10 minutes, until topping is golden and crisp. Serve warm or at room temperature.

Empanadillas with Tuna

Serves 4

2 tablespoons (40 ml/1½ fl oz)
olive oil

1 tablespoon chopped onion

100 g (3½ oz) canned tuna
in brine, drained and flaked

2 tablespoons sliced,
pimento-stuffed olives

½ teaspoon sweet Spanish
paprika

1 tablespoon finely chopped
flat-leaf parsley

salt and freshly ground black
pepper

250 g (9 oz) ready-rolled puff
pastry

1 egg yolk, beaten, to glaze

Heat oil in a non-stick pan over medium heat. Add onion and cook for 4–5 minutes, stirring occasionally, until softened. Add tuna, olives, paprika and parsley, then cook, stirring, for about 5 minutes. Check seasoning and add salt and pepper if needed. Leave to cool.

Preheat the oven to 190°C (375°F). Line two baking trays with baking paper.

Cut pastry into 7.5-cm (3-in) circles and arrange on baking trays. Place a teaspoon of the tuna mixture on each round and fold the pastry over to form a crescent shape. Press the edges with a fork, or pinch together with your finger, to seal. Brush the tops with beaten egg yolk, and bake in preheated oven for 12–15 minutes, until golden brown. Serve warm.

Salt Cod Purée

Brandada de bacalao

Serves 4–6

500 g (1 lb 2 oz) salt cod,
  soaked (see page 4)

2 cups (500 ml/17 fl oz) milk

4 black peppercorns

2 sprigs fresh parsley

2 bay leaves

2 cloves garlic, chopped

juice of 1 lemon

1 cup (250 ml/8½ oz) olive oil

750 g (1 lb 10 oz) potatoes,
  boiled and mashed

3 tablespoons chopped flat-leaf
  parsley

freshly ground black pepper

Place soaked cod in a large saucepan with the milk, peppercorns, parsley, bay leaves and enough water to cover. Poach gently for 15–20 minutes or until the fish is soft and flaky. Reserve about 3 tablespoons (60 ml/2 fl oz) of the poaching liquid. Remove fish carefully from the pan, flake fish and discard bones and skin (make sure there are no small bones left). Put fish into a blender or food processor with garlic and lemon juice. Drizzle in the oil and pulse until you have a thick purée. Add potatoes and parsley, and pulse again until just combined (add a little of the reserved poaching liquid if mixture is too stiff – it should be creamy and light). Season with pepper.

Serve at room temperature, piled onto crisp toast or as a filling for piquillo peppers. The purée will keep, refrigerated, for 2–3 days.

Fried Squid

Calamares fritos

Serves 4

500 g (1 lb 2 oz) squid tubes,
sliced into 1-cm (⅜-in) rings

1½ cups (150 g/5 oz) plain
flour

2 teaspoons sweet Spanish
paprika

salt and freshly ground black
pepper

olive oil for deep-frying

2 lemons, cut into wedges,
to serve

alioli (page 238), to serve

Pat squid rings dry with paper towel.

Mix flour and paprika in a bowl and season with salt and pepper. Toss squid rings in flour until lightly dusted, shaking off any excess.

Heat the oil in a deep, heavy-based saucepan until very hot. To test, drop in a cube of bread – it should sizzle and turn brown within a few seconds.

Add the squid rings, a few at a time, and cook for about 2 minutes, until golden brown. Remove with a slotted spoon and drain on paper towel.

Serve hot, with lemon wedges alongside and alioli for dipping.

✕ Cuttlefish pieces are commonly cooked this way too.

Salt Cod Fritters

Bunuelos de bacalao

Serves 6

500 g (1 lb 2 oz) salt cod,
  soaked (see page 4)

2 cups (500 ml/17 fl oz) milk

3 tablespoons (60 ml/2 fl oz)
  olive oil

1 onion, finely chopped

2 cloves garlic, chopped

500 g (1 lb 2 oz) potatoes,
  boiled and mashed

2 eggs, beaten

2 tablespoons finely chopped
  flat-leaf parsley

salt and freshly ground black
  pepper

olive oil for frying

lemon wedges, and alioli
  (page 238), to serve

Drain the cod, pat dry, and cut into large pieces.

Heat the milk in a large saucepan or deep frying pan over medium heat. Add the cod, and bring to the boil, reduce the heat and simmer very gently for about 30 minutes, until the fish is soft. Drain, and leave to cool.

Flake the fish, removing any skin or bones, then mash with a fork.

Heat the oil in a frying pan, add onion and garlic, and cook over medium heat for a few minutes until softened.

Put mashed potato in a bowl, add mashed cod, cooked onion and garlic, beaten eggs and parsley, and stir together with a wooden spoon.

Season with salt and pepper to taste (you probably won't need salt, as there will be some from the cod). Shape mixture into small patties and refrigerate for at least 30 minutes until firm.

Heat about 4 cm (1½ in) oil in a large heavy-based frying pan over medium heat until very hot. Add patties, a few at a time, and cook for 3–4 minutes, turning once, until golden brown.

Drain on paper towel and serve hot with alioli and lemon wedges.

Chickpeas & Chorizo

Serves 4

200 g (7 oz) dried chickpeas

4 cloves

1 cinnamon stick

3 tablespoons (60 ml/2 fl oz) olive oil

1 clove garlic, crushed

1 small onion, finely chopped

350 g (12 oz) cured chorizo, cut into small cubes

2 tablespoons (40 ml/1½ fl oz) dry sherry (optional)

salt and freshly ground black pepper

⅓ cup chopped fresh flat-leaf parsley

Soak chickpeas in cold water overnight. Drain, then put in a saucepan and cover with fresh cold water. Add the cloves and cinnamon stick. Bring to boil and simmer covered for 45 minutes or until tender. Add a little more water if needed during cooking. Drain.

Heat the oil in a large non-stick frying pan over medium heat. Add garlic and onion and sauté, stirring occasionally, until softened. Add chorizo and sauté for 2–3 minutes until lightly browned and heated through. Add drained chickpeas and sherry (if using), then stir for a few minutes until heated through. Season to taste. Sprinkle with chopped parsley and serve.

※ You can use canned chickpeas (400-g/14-oz can): if so, drain, rinse, add fresh water, cloves and cinnamon, and simmer for 5 minutes before adding to the pan.

Garlic & Chilli Mushrooms

Serves 4

2 tablespoons (40 ml/1½ fl oz)
olive oil

5 cloves garlic, crushed

250 g (9 oz) button
mushrooms, stems trimmed

4 tablespoons (80 ml/3 fl oz)
dry sherry

2 tablespoons (40 ml/1½ fl oz)
freshly squeezed lemon juice

1 small dried red chilli,
crushed

¼ teaspoon sweet or hot
Spanish paprika

salt and freshly ground black
pepper

½ cup finely chopped fresh
flat-leaf parsley

Heat oil in a large, non-stick frying pan over medium heat. When hot, add garlic and sauté for about 1 minute (don't let it burn).

Add the mushrooms, sherry, lemon juice, chilli and paprika. Cook, stirring, for 4–5 minutes, until mushrooms soften. Add a little extra oil if the mixture seems too dry (but remember that the mushrooms will gradually release moisture).

Season with salt and pepper to taste and stir chopped parsley through. Serve warm or at room temperature.

Chorizo in Red Wine

Serves 4–6

600 g (1 lb 5 oz) fresh chorizo

2 cups (500 ml/17 fl oz) light red wine (a Rioja or a pinot noir are good)

6–8 black peppercorns, roughly crushed

2 sprigs fresh rosemary

olive oil for frying

1 tablespoon finely chopped flat-leaf parsley, to serve

Prick chorizos all over. Place in a bowl, pour wine over, and add peppercorns and rosemary. Cover, and marinate for 24 hours. Drain.

Lightly oil a barbecue grill or large non-stick frying pan, and preheat to medium. Cook chorizos over a medium heat for 6–8 minutes, until surfaces are crispy. Slice into thick diagonal chunks.

Arrange chorizos on a platter, scatter with fresh parsley and serve immediately.

Fava Bean Omelette

Serves 4

300 g (10½ oz) fresh broad
  beans, shelled

3 tablespoons (60 ml/2 fl oz)
  olive oil

1 small onion, chopped

2 cloves garlic, chopped

6 eggs

salt and freshly ground black
  pepper

70 g (2½ oz) Swiss cheese,
  grated

Cook the beans in boiling water for 4–5 minutes, until soft. Drain, rinse under cold water and drain again. Remove the outer skins to reveal the bright-green seed.

Heat 2 tablespoons (40 ml/1½ fl oz) of the oil in a non-stick frying pan. Add the onion and garlic and cook for 3–4 minutes, until onion is softened.

Beat eggs lightly with salt and pepper. Add cooked onion and beans, and the cheese, and stir through.

Heat the remaining oil in frying pan over medium heat. Add egg mixture, lower heat and cook gently until set. Serve warm or at room temperature, cut into small pieces for tapas, or in wedges served with salad as a light meal.

※ Fava is another name for broad beans. You can use frozen beans for this recipe if fresh are not available, but dried beans are not suitable.

Jamon-wrapped Fish

Serves 4–6

500 g (1 lb 2 oz) firm white
fish fillets

1 tablespoon hot Spanish
paprika

12 slices jamon (or prosciutto),
sliced into wide strips

2 tablespoons (40 ml/1½ fl oz)
extra-virgin olive oil

freshly ground black pepper

lemon wedges, to serve

Preheat grill to high.

Cut fish into bite-sized pieces. Sprinkle a little paprika on each piece,
then wrap in a strip of jamon and secure with a toothpick.

Put fish parcels under the grill for 8–10 minutes, turning once or twice,
until the fish is cooked through. Transfer to a warmed platter, drizzle with
oil, and season with black pepper. Serve immediately, with lemon wedges.

Catalan Bread with Tomato

Pa amb tomaquet

Serves 4

4 slices firm, good-quality
  bread

2 cloves garlic,
  cut in half lengthways

2 vine-ripened tomatoes,
  peeled and thickly sliced

extra-virgin olive oil
  for drizzling

salt and freshly ground black
  pepper

Lightly toast the bread, or grill over a wood-fired barbecue for a smoky taste.
Cut each slice in half and rub with garlic.

Mash one slice of tomato and spread a little on each of the toast slices.
Lay the remaining tomato slices on top, drizzle with oil, season with salt and
pepper, and serve.

✕ This is a very popular tapa, or a snack at any time. Use ripe, full-
flavoured tomatoes and top-quality olive oil. Catalans often add jamon,
cheese, anchovies or other toppings with the tomato.

Jamon Iberico with Asparagus

Serves 4

12 asparagus spears,
  ends trimmed

150 g (5 oz) thinly sliced
  jamon Iberico

2 tablespoons (40 ml/1½ fl oz)
  olive oil

freshly ground black pepper

½ cup (160 g/5½ oz) romesco
  sauce (page 240)

Cook asparagus in boiling water for 3–4 minutes until just starting to soften but still bright green. Drain, then plunge asparagus into iced water to stop the cooking. Drain well. Pat dry, then wrap each spear in a piece of jamon (leave the tips showing).

Heat the oil in a non-stick frying pan, and when hot add the jamon-wrapped asparagus. Fry for 2–3 minutes until jamon starts to crisp. Drain quickly on paper towel, season with pepper and serve immediately with romesco sauce for dipping.

※ Jamon Iberico, considered the king of jamon, is eaten in the simplest way, either with fresh bread or, as here, with seasonal asparagus. If you cannot buy this ham, use jamon serrano or prosciutto instead.

Ham Croquettes

Croquetas de jamon

Serves 6

3 tablespoons (60 g/2 oz) unsalted butter

3 tablespoons (45 g/1½ oz) plain flour

2 cups (500 ml/17 fl oz) milk

100 g (3½ oz) jamon serrano, chopped

½ teaspoon ground nutmeg

salt and freshly ground black pepper

plain flour, for dusting

2 eggs, lightly beaten

1 cup dried breadcrumbs

oil for deep-frying

Heat the butter in a heavy-based saucepan over medium heat, then stir in the flour and cook for 1 minute, stirring. Gradually add the milk and continue stirring for a few minutes, until the mixture forms a thick sauce. Remove from heat.

Stir jamon and nutmeg into the sauce. Check seasoning and add salt and pepper to taste. Leave to cool a little.

Pour croquette mixture into a baking dish. Cover and refrigerate for 2–3 hours, or overnight, until mixture is set.

Use a spoon to scoop out small amounts of mixture, then shape these into egg-shaped croquettes. Coat each croquette lightly in flour. Then dip into beaten egg, and lastly the breadcrumbs. Place croquettes on a tray and refrigerate for at least 30 minutes. >

Heat about 5 cm (2 in) of oil in a heavy-based saucepan over medium–high heat. Deep-fry croquettes in small batches until golden on all sides. Remove with a slotted spoon and drain on paper towel. Keep warm until all the croquettes are cooked.

Serve immediately.

✕ If you have time, make the mixture the day before assembling the croquettes as it will be easier to handle.

Eggs with Tuna

Huevos con atun

Makes 16

8 hard-boiled eggs, shelled

100 g (3½ oz) canned tuna in brine or springwater, drained and mashed

4 tablespoons (100 g/3 oz) good-quality mayonnaise

2 tablespoons (50 g/1¾ oz) Dijon mustard

1 tablespoon (20 ml/¾ fl oz) freshly squeezed lemon juice

½ teaspoon sweet Spanish paprika, plus extra to serve

salt, to taste

finely chopped flat-leaf parsley, for garnish

Halve the eggs lengthways and scoop out yolks. Set whites aside. Mash yolks with the tuna, then add the mayonnaise, mustard, lemon juice, paprika and salt, mixing well.

Pile the tuna mixture into the egg-white halves. Cover and refrigerate until ready to serve.

To serve, sprinkle with parsley and dust with a little extra paprika if desired.

Kidneys with Sherry

Rinones al Jerez

Serves 4

2 veal kidneys

2 tablespoons (40 ml/1½ fl oz) sherry vinegar

2 tablespoons (40 ml/1½ fl oz) olive oil

1 clove garlic, crushed

1 teaspoon hot or sweet Spanish paprika

1 sprig fresh thyme

1 tablespoon chopped flat-leaf parsley

½ cup (125 ml/4 fl oz) dry sherry

½ cup (125 ml/4 fl oz) veal stock

salt and freshly ground black pepper

1 tablespoon fresh breadcrumbs

Skin kidneys and cut out the core, then slice thinly. Place in a ceramic or glass dish, cover with ¼ cup (60 ml/2 fl oz) water and the sherry vinegar, and leave to soak for 30 minutes. Drain well and pat dry with paper towel.

Heat the oil in a heavy-based pan over medium heat, add garlic and sauté for 1 minute until just soft. Add kidney slices and cook for 2–3 minutes, turning once, until seared. Add paprika, thyme and parsley, then pour in the sherry and cook for 1 minute. Add veal stock to pan, season with salt and pepper, and cover. Reduce heat and simmer for 15–20 minutes, checking occasionally, until kidneys are soft. Gently stir in the breadcrumbs until sauce thickens a little. Check seasoning and serve hot.

Padron Peppers

Serves 4

500 g (1 lb 2 oz) padron peppers

2–3 (40–60 ml/1–2 fl oz)
   tablespoons olive oil

salt flakes

Wash peppers and pat dry. Leave whole, with stems attached (to hold when eating).

Heat the oil in a heavy-based frying pan and when hot, toss in the peppers and sauté, turning so that they are coated in the oil. Cook for a few minutes, turning until they are lightly blistered and starting to soften.

Transfer to a warmed serving plate, sprinkle generously with salt and serve immediately.

※ Padron peppers are small green chillies that are usually – but not always – mild. About one in every ten is extremely hot, so beware!

Fried Black Pudding

Morcilla frita

Makes 10

1 tablespoon (20 ml/¾ fl oz) olive oil

1 clove garlic, sliced

1 red onion, finely chopped

1 teaspoon sweet Spanish paprika

1 sprig fresh oregano

250 g (9 oz) black pudding (*morcilla*), cut into 10 slices

10 slices crusty breadstick, cut on the angle

2 tablespoons (40 ml/1½ fl oz) dry sherry

salt and freshly ground black pepper

Heat the oil in a large frying pan over medium heat, then add the garlic, onion, paprika and oregano, and sauté for 3–4 minutes, until onion is softened.

Add black pudding and cook for about 4 minutes, turning once or twice, until lightly browned. Put a piece of black pudding on each slice of bread and arrange on a serving plate.

Add sherry to pan, season with salt and pepper, and heat through. Drizzle a little of the sauce over the black pudding and serve immediately.

Paprika-spiced Almonds

Serves 6

2 tablespoons (40 ml/1½ fl oz)
extra-virgin olive oil

500 g (1 lb 2 oz) blanched
almonds

1 teaspoon hot Spanish
paprika

1 teaspoon ground cumin

1 tablespoon salt flakes

Heat the oil in a frying pan over medium heat. Add almonds and cook,
stirring, for about 5 minutes or until they are golden brown.

Add paprika and cumin to pan and stir to coat almonds. Remove from the
heat and add salt flakes. Serve warm or cold.

Piquillos with Anchovies

Serves 4–6

10–12 anchovy fillets in oil,
  drained

220 g (8 oz) pickled piquillo
  peppers, sliced

extra-virgin olive oil for
  drizzling

2 tablespoons finely chopped
  flat-leaf parsley

crusty bread or triangles of
  toast, to serve

If anchovy fillets are long, cut them in half.

Arrange pepper slices on a platter, then lay anchovy fillets on top. Drizzle a little oil over the dish and sprinkle with chopped parsley.

Serve at room temperature, with crusty bread or toast.

※ Piquillo peppers are a variety of red chilli, which are sweet rather than hot. Roasted, peeled and pickled, they are available in jars and cans from specialist food stores.

Pork Skewers

Pinchitos

Serves 4

3 cloves garlic, chopped

1 teaspoon sea salt

½ teaspoon each of hot
Spanish paprika, coriander,
cumin, turmeric, cardamom
and fenugreek

pinch of saffron threads

freshly ground black pepper

1 tablespoon (20 ml/¾ fl oz)
freshly squeezed lemon juice

3 tablespoons (50 ml/2 fl oz)
olive oil

500 g (1 lb 2 oz) lean pork,
cut into small cubes

lemon wedges, to serve

You will need 4–6 bamboo skewers, soaked in cold water for at least 1 hour. Crush garlic and salt in a mortar, then add spices, lemon juice and oil, and grind to a paste.

Thread pork onto skewers. Place skewers in a shallow dish and coat with the spice paste. Cover and refrigerate for 2–3 hours.

Preheat grill or barbecue to high. Grill skewers for about 4 minutes, turning once or twice, until cooked.

Transfer to a warmed plate and serve with lemon wedges on the side.

✖ These small, spicy pork kebabs reflect Moorish influences. Pinchito spice mix is available in some specialist food stores: this recipe includes many of the spices in the traditional blend.

Pork Rolls with Jamon Serrano

Serves 8

8 boneless pork cutlets, about
   1.5 cm (½ in) thick

freshly ground black pepper

8 thin slices jamon serrano

2 eggs

2 tablespoons (40 ml/1½ fl oz)
   milk

1 cup dry breadcrumbs

oil for frying

alioli (page 238) or
   mayonnaise, to serve

Pound cutlets with a rolling pin or mallet until flattened and about twice
their original diameter. Season with pepper, then lay a slice of jamon on
each cutlet. Roll up tightly (secure with a toothpick if necessary).

Lightly whisk eggs and milk. Dip each cutlet into the egg mixture, then into
the breadcrumbs, pressing to make sure rolls are well coated.

Heat oil to a depth of about 2 cm (¾ in) in a heavy-based frying pan over
medium heat. When hot, but not smoking, add rolls in batches and fry for
about 5–6 minutes, turning carefully to make sure they are golden and crisp
on all sides. Remove from pan and drain on paper towel. Keep warm until
all rolls are cooked.

Cut rolls in thick slices on the angle and serve hot or warm, with alioli or
mayonnaise on the side.

Fried Cheese

Queso frito

Makes about 20

250 g manchego cheese (or use provolone or mozzarella)

plain flour, for dusting

2 eggs, lightly beaten

1 cup dry breadcrumbs

salt and freshly ground black pepper

olive oil for deep-frying

1 tablespoon chopped fresh dill, and lemon wedges, to serve

Cut cheese into sticks about 1 cm (3/8 in) thick and 5 cm (2 in) long. Dust lightly with flour, dip into beaten egg and then into the breadcrumbs. Place cheese sticks on a plate, cover and refrigerate for at least 1 hour until coating is firm.

Pour about 5 cm (2 in) oil into a heavy-based saucepan and place over medium heat until hot. Fry cheese sticks a few at a time. Remove with slotted spoon and drain on paper towel. Keep warm until all are cooked.

Serve immediately, sprinkled with fresh dill, with lemon wedges on the side.

※ To ensure the cheese sticks are crisp on the outside and soft inside, keep the oil hot (170°C/340°F) but do not let it start smoking. If the oil gets too hot, remove from the heat for a minute or two.

Quince & Blue Cheese Montaditos

Makes 12

12 thick slices good-quality
  breadstick, cut on an angle

2 tablespoons (40 ml/1½ fl oz)
  extra-virgin olive oil

3 cloves garlic, halved

100 g (4 oz) quince paste

100 g (4 oz) soft blue-vein
  cheese

Preheat oven to 180°C (360°F).

Brush both sides of the bread slices with oil and rub with garlic. Place on baking tray in preheated oven and cook for 5 minutes, turning once, until toasted and golden. Remove from oven and allow to cool.

Place a slice of quince paste on each toast. Top with blue cheese and serve.

※ A montadito is similar to Italian bruschetta – basically a slice of toast with a savoury topping.

Spiced Olives

Makes about 2 cups

1 teaspoon fennel seeds

1 tablespoon cumin seeds

1 tablespoon coriander seeds

⅓ cup (80 ml/3 fl oz) olive oil

3 cloves garlic, finely sliced

1 tablespoon dried red chilli
flakes

1 tablespoon finely grated
lemon zest

500 g (1 lb 2 oz) mixed olives
(black and green)

½ cup finely chopped flat-leaf
parsley

Place fennel, cumin and coriander seeds in a frying pan over medium heat and toast until lightly browned and fragrant.

Heat oil in a small pan until just warm. Add garlic, chilli flakes, toasted seeds and lemon zest, and stir over medium heat for 2–3 minutes, to infuse oil.

Place olives in a bowl, pour warmed oil over and stir to coat. Cover with cling wrap and leave at room temperature to marinate for at least a few hours before serving. Stir occasionally.

Stir chopped parsley through before serving.

✳ To keep the olives for 3–4 weeks, store in a clean, sterilised jar in the refrigerator. Use a clean spoon when removing olives from the jar.

Anchovy & Olive Sticks

Gildas

Makes 10

20 pitted green olives

**10 pickled piquillo peppers,
cut into strips**

10 anchovies in oil, drained

Thread an olive, a strip of pepper and a folded anchovy onto a toothpick then finish with another green olive. Repeat with remaining ingredients. Arrange on a plate and serve.

✕ These small, salty morsels are a favourite at tapas bars. The word *gilda* means lollipop.

Spinach Empanadas

Serves 4

3 tablespoons (60 ml/2 fl oz) olive oil

3 cloves garlic, crushed

250 g (9 oz) vine-ripened tomatoes, chopped

pinch of Spanish paprika

750 g (1 lb 10 oz) spinach, rinsed and chopped

½ cup pine nuts, lightly toasted

2 hard-boiled eggs, shelled and chopped

salt and freshly ground black pepper

2 sheets ready-rolled short-crust pastry

1 egg, lightly beaten

Heat oil in a frying pan. Add garlic and sauté for 1–2 minutes until soft. Add tomatoes and paprika, and cook for 10–15 minutes over low heat, stirring occasionally, until mixture thickens into a sauce. Add spinach and pine nuts, stir through and cook until spinach is wilted. The mixture should be fairly dry; if not, cook over high heat to reduce. Stir chopped egg through mixture and season to taste.

Preheat oven to 180°C (360°F). Line two baking trays with baking paper. Cut pastry into 12-cm (5-in) rounds. Spoon a little filling into centre of each pastry, then fold over and pinch to seal edges. Brush lightly with beaten egg and bake for 15–20 minutes, until golden brown. Serve hot or at room temperature.

Fried Spanish Olives

Serves 4

40 g (1½ oz) soft goat's cheese

250 g (9 oz) large, pitted green Spanish olives, drained

¾ cup fresh breadcrumbs

½ cup finely grated parmesan cheese

¼ teaspoon hot Spanish paprika

1 egg, beaten with 1 tablespoon (20 ml/¾ fl oz) water

⅓ cup (50 g/1¾ oz) plain flour

olive oil for deep-frying

Line a baking tray or flat plate with baking paper. Stuff a little of the goat's cheese into each olive, using a small spoon.

Mix together breadcrumbs, parmesan and paprika. Dip olives in flour to dust lightly, then into the beaten egg and, finally, the breadcrumbs. Place on prepared tray or plate. When all the olives are crumbed, refrigerate for 15–30 minutes.

Heat about 4 cm (1½ in) oil in a heavy-based saucepan over medium–high heat. To test, drop in a small cube of bread – it should sizzle and turn brown within a few seconds. Fry olives in batches until golden, then remove with a slotted spoon and drain on paper towel. Repeat with the remaining olives.

Serve immediately.

Cheese & Fig Open Sandwich

Montaditos de manchego

Serves 8

16 thick slices firm breadstick,
cut on the angle

100 g (4 oz) butter, softened

2 tablespoons (60 g/2 oz)
fig jam

8 slices jamon

100 g (4 oz) manchego cheese,
pared into thin slices

extra-virgin olive oil, to serve

freshly ground black pepper

Preheat the oven to 150°C (300°F). Place bread slices on a tray in the oven and bake for 8–10 minutes, turning once, until golden on both sides.

Mix butter and fig jam, and spread on the prepared toasts. Top with jamon and cheese slices. Drizzle with a little oil, season with black pepper, and serve.

✕ If manchego is not available, you could use another semi-hard cheese such as gruyère.

Olive, Anchovy & Caper Puffs

Serves 4

1 tablespoon baby capers,
rinsed

4 canned anchovy fillets in oil,
drained and chopped

3 tablespoons (90 g/3 oz)
Spanish tapenade (page 242)

2 tablespoons finely chopped
flat-leaf parsley

2 sheets ready-rolled puff
pastry

Preheat the oven to 210°C (410°F). Line two trays with baking paper.

Put capers, anchovies, tapenade and parsley in a small bowl and mix well. Spread half the mixture onto one sheet of pastry, roll up pastry firmly to form a log, pressing well to seal the edge. Using a sharp knife, cut into 2-cm (¾-in) slices and place flat on prepared baking tray.

Repeat with remaining mixture and the other pastry sheet.

Place pastries in preheated oven and bake for 5–6 minutes, until puffed and golden. Transfer to a warmed serving plate and serve.

Soups & Stews

Spain's most famous soup is undoubtedly gazpacho; a chilled, tomato-based mixture. It comes in numerous regional guises, some smooth, some chunky, but all refreshing in the country's often searingly hot summers. A less familiar, delicate version is the 'white' gazpacho – the almond-based *ajo blanco*, typically garnished with cool green grapes and crisp croutons.

Other traditional soups and stews are much more substantial – rich broths laden with seafood, or sustaining peasant fare; hearty with meat, vegetables, and, of course, flavoured with smoky Spanish paprika.

‹ Almond Gazpacho (page 62)

Almond Gazpacho

Ajo blanco

Serves 4–6

6 slices firm, stale white bread, crusts removed

2 cloves garlic, crushed

1 teaspoon salt flakes

100 g (3½ oz) blanched almonds

½ cup (125 ml/4 fl oz) extra-virgin olive oil

¼ cup (60 ml/2 fl oz) dry sherry

1½ cups (375 ml/12½ fl oz) vegetable stock

1 cup seedless green grapes, washed, stems removed

1 cup croutons (see note next page)

Soak bread in a small amount of cold water until soft, then squeeze out excess moisture.

Pound garlic and salt in a mortar to form a paste. Blend paste with almonds in a food processor until almonds are finely ground. Add the soaked bread and process again, then pour in oil in a thin steady stream until mixture thickens. Add sherry and stock and continue to blend. The soup should be smooth.

Cover and refrigerate for 2–3 hours.

Check seasoning before serving – it may need extra salt. If soup is too thick, add a little iced water.

Pour into individual bowls, scatter with grapes (cut them in half if they are large) and croutons, and serve.

✕ Bread is often used to thicken Spanish soups, either soaked and pounded to a paste, or added as crumbs or in pieces and stirred through. To make croutons, cut stale crusty bread into small cubes. Fry in hot oil for about 2 minutes, or until golden and crisp, then drain on paper towel.

Chickpea & Cod Soup

Serves 6

5 tablespoons (160 ml/5½ fl oz)
  olive oil

1 onion, chopped

500 g (1 lb 2 oz) chickpeas,
  soaked overnight, drained

1 bay leaf

250 g (9 oz) salt cod, soaked
  (see page 4), cut into bite-
  sized pieces

250 g (9 oz) potatoes, peeled
  and finely chopped

2 cloves garlic, chopped

1 tablespoon finely chopped
  flat-leaf parsley

½ teaspoon ground cumin

½ teaspoon mild Spanish
  paprika

1 bunch spinach, leaves rinsed
  and chopped

salt and freshly ground black
  pepper

Heat 2 tablespoons (40 ml/1½ fl oz) of the oil in a heavy-based saucepan until hot, then sauté onion for 3–4 minutes, stirring occasionally, until it is transparent. Add chickpeas and bay leaf, pour in 2 litres (4 pt 4 fl oz) water and bring to boil. Cover pan, reduce heat and simmer for about 45 minutes, removing any scum from the surface, until chickpeas are starting to soften.

Add cod and cook for another 30 minutes. Add potatoes and cook for a further 15 minutes, until vegetables and chickpeas are soft.

Meanwhile, pound remaining oil, garlic, parsley, cumin and paprika in a mortar to form a rough paste.

Stir chopped spinach into soup and heat through. Check for seasoning, adding salt and pepper to taste.

To serve, ladle soup into warmed bowls and top each with a scoop of the parsley paste.

✕ You will need to start this recipe a day ahead, to allow for soaking the chickpeas and the salted cod.

Galician Fish Soup

Serves 4

1.5 kg (3 lb 5 oz) fresh mixed
   seafood (see note page 68),
   cleaned

⅓ cup (80 ml/3 fl oz) olive oil

2 onions, thinly sliced

1 clove garlic, crushed

2 tablespoons chopped flat-leaf
   parsley

1 tablespoon sweet Spanish
   paprika

1 small fresh red chilli, sliced,
   seeds removed

salt

½ cup (125 ml/4 fl oz) dry
   white wine

freshly ground black pepper

CROUTONS

2 slices day-old sourdough
   bread, lightly toasted

a little extra-virgin olive oil

Pat fish dry, then slice into generous, bite-sized pieces. Remove shells from crustaceans. Place seafood in a large saucepan or stockpot, with the oil, onion, garlic, half the parsley, the paprika and the red chilli. Sprinkle with salt, cover and leave for 30 minutes.

Add enough water to the pan to cover the seafood completely. Bring to the boil, then add the wine, cover and simmer for 15–20 minutes.

To make the croutons, cut toast into 4 triangles and brush with olive oil. ❯

Check soup for seasoning and add pepper if needed. Put a crouton in the bottom of each serving bowl, place a few pieces of seafood on top and ladle the broth over at once. Sprinkle with chopped parsley and serve.

✕ For this stew-like soup, choose very small fish such as red mullet or hake, shellfish such as crab or prawns, and baby squid. If using mussels, scrub shells and add them to the soup in the last 5 minutes of cooking. Discard any mussels whose shells do not open.

Garlic Soup

Serves 6

5 tablespoons (100 m/3½ fl oz) olive oil

6 cloves garlic, peeled

12 thin slices firm breadstick, crusts removed

6 eggs

1 teaspoon Spanish paprika

1.5 litres (3 pt 3 fl oz) chicken or vegetable stock

salt and freshly ground black pepper

2 tablespoons finely chopped flat-leaf parsley

Preheat oven to 180°C (360°F). Place 6 ovenproof bowls on a baking tray.

Heat oil in a large, non-stick saucepan over medium heat. Add garlic and sauté for a few minutes. Remove garlic from pan and set aside.

Add slices of bread to pan in batches, and sauté until golden on both sides (add a little extra oil if needed). Put a piece of fried bread in the base of each soup bowl. Break an egg onto each slice.

Return garlic to the pan, add paprika and stock, season with salt and pepper and bring to the boil, then ladle broth over carefully.

Place tray in preheated oven and cook for about 5 minutes, until the egg-white is set but the yolk is still runny. Remove from oven, sprinkle with parsley and serve.

Spanish Tomato Soup with Goat's Cheese Toasts

Serves 6

⅓ cup (80 ml/3 fl oz) olive oil

1 red onion, chopped

2 cloves garlic, sliced

1 red capsicum, deseeded and chopped

2 kg (4 lb 6 oz) vine-ripened tomatoes, peeled and chopped

1 teaspoon sweet Spanish paprika

1 teaspoon ground cumin

salt and freshly ground black pepper

6 thin slices of firm breadstick, lightly toasted

60 g (2 oz) soft goat's cheese

Heat about 3 tablespoons (60 ml/2 fl oz) of the oil in a large, heavy-based saucepan over low heat. Add onion, garlic and capsicum and cook, stirring occasionally, for about 10 minutes until vegetables are quite soft.

Add tomatoes, paprika and cumin, cover pan and simmer for 20 minutes. Allow soup to cool a little, then blend in batches until smooth.

Return soup to heat, season with salt and pepper, and reheat.

Brush toasted breadstick slices with oil, then spread with goat's cheese. Pour soup into warmed bowls, top each with a prepared toast and serve immediately.

Lentil & Pork Soup

Serves 4–6

3 tablespoons (60 ml/2 fl oz) olive oil

2 cloves garlic, crushed

2 sticks celery, thickly sliced

2 medium-sized carrots, thickly sliced

2 boneless pork loin chops, cut into cubes

4 medium-sized potatoes, peeled and cut into small cubes

500 g (1 lb 2 oz) dried brown lentils, rinsed

½ teaspoon ground cumin

salt and freshly ground black pepper

Heat oil in a large, heavy-based, non-stick saucepan over medium heat. Add garlic and sauté for 1 minute. Add celery and carrots, sauté again for a few minutes, then add cubed pork and sauté for a few minutes more, until meat is lightly browned all over.

Add potatoes, lentils and cumin, then add enough water to cover meat and vegetables. Bring to boil, cover, reduce heat and simmer for 40–50 minutes. Stir occasionally, and add a little extra water if needed. When soup is quite thick and lentils are soft, season with salt and pepper. Serve hot with crusty bread.

※ Lentils and other pulses frequently feature in Spanish soups and stews. If you prefer, you can leave out the pork – this still makes a substantial dish.

Gazpacho Andalucia

Serve 4–6

2 cloves garlic, crushed

1 teaspoon salt

1 slice firm, day-old bread, crusts removed

750 g (1 lb 10 oz) vine-ripened tomatoes, roughly chopped

2 Lebanese cucumbers, deseeded and chopped

1 green capsicum, deseeded and roughly chopped

2 tablespoons (40 ml/1½ fl oz) red-wine vinegar

⅓ cup (80 ml/3 fl oz) extra-virgin olive oil

salt and freshly ground black pepper

1 cup croutons (see note page 63), to serve

extra Lebanese cucumber, deseeded and finely chopped, to serve

2 hard-boiled eggs, shelled and chopped, to serve

Pound garlic and salt in a mortar until it forms a paste. Soak bread in water until softened, then squeeze to remove excess moisture.

Put garlic paste, soaked bread, tomato, cucumber, capsicum and vinegar in food processor and process until blended to your preferred texture (from smooth to chunky). Pour oil in slowly and continue blending. Season with pepper and extra salt if needed.

Cover and refrigerate for 2–3 hours until well chilled. Serve with small bowls of croutons, cucumber and hard-boiled eggs on the side.

Rustic Squid Stew

Serves 4

3 tablespoons (60 ml/2 fl oz) olive oil

750 g squid (1 lb 10 oz), cleaned and cut into rings (leave tentacles in one piece if not too long)

1 red onion, finely chopped

2 cloves garlic, crushed

400 g (14 oz) canned chopped tomatoes

1 small fresh red chilli, deseeded and sliced

1¾ cups (435 ml/15 fl oz) fish stock

1 teaspoon sweet Spanish paprika

1 bay leaf

salt and freshly ground black pepper

2 tablespoons finely chopped flat-leaf parsley, to serve

Heat oil in a large, heavy-based pan over high heat. Add squid and cook, stirring occasionally, until golden brown.

Add onion and garlic and cook for 6–7 minutes, stirring occasionally, until transparent and starting to caramelise. Add tomatoes, chilli, stock, paprika and bay leaf and bring to the boil. Cover, reduce heat to very low and simmer for 2 hours. Remove the bay leaf, check for seasoning and add salt and pepper if needed. Spoon into warmed bowls, scatter with parsley and serve.

✕ For squid to be tender, it must be cooked very quickly or very slowly. This slow-simmer method results in a melt-in-the-mouth texture.

White Bean & Sausage Stew

Fabada Asturiana

Serves 6–8

900 g (2 lb) dried broad beans,
    or cannellini beans, soaked
    overnight

450 g (1 lb) salt pork
    or ham hock

6 cloves garlic, halved

6 peppercorns, roughly
    crushed

1 teaspoon sweet Spanish
    paprika

350 g (12 oz) fresh chorizo,
    whole

350 g (12 oz) black pudding
    (*morcilla*), whole

finely chopped flat-leaf parsley

Drain beans and put in a large, heavy-based saucepan. Add pork, garlic, peppercorns, paprika, chorizo and black pudding. Fill with cold water to cover by about 2.5 cm (1 in). Bring to boil over medium heat, then reduce heat, cover and cook for about 1 hour. Check occasionally, stirring gently. Add more water, if necessary, to keep ingredients covered. After 1 hour, add salt to taste and continue simmering until beans are soft. (Don't boil, or beans may split and lose their skins.)

Remove from heat and leave for 5–10 minutes. Remove meats from the pan and slice thickly. Arrange meats in warmed bowls, then spoon beans onto plates and ladle on some of the broth. Scatter with chopped parsley and serve.

✕ Traditionally, the meat is served separately from the broth and beans, but you can serve together if you wish.

Gypsy Stew

Olla Gitana

Serves 6

800g (1 lb 12 oz) canned chickpeas, rinsed and drained

250 g (9 oz) green beans, trimmed and cut into 5-cm (2-in) lengths

400 g (14 oz) pumpkin, peeled and chopped

2 litres (4 pt 4 fl oz) good-quality chicken or vegetable stock

small bunch spinach, washed and chopped

salt and freshly ground black pepper

about 3 tablespoons (60 ml/2 fl oz) olive oil

2 cloves garlic, chopped

12 blanched almonds, chopped

1 piece stale, firm white bread, crusts removed, cut into cubes

2 medium-sized, vine-ripened tomatoes, peeled and chopped

2 pears, not too ripe, peeled and cut into small cubes

1 teaspoon sweet Spanish paprika

1 tablespoon (20 ml/¾ fl oz) sherry vinegar

a few threads saffron, crumbled, and then soaked in a little warm water

Put chickpeas, beans and pumpkin in a large, heavy-based saucepan, add the stock, bring to the boil and simmer, uncovered, for about 10–15 minutes until vegetables are cooked.

Stir chopped spinach into pan and season to taste with salt and pepper. >

Heat two-thirds of the oil in a frying pan over medium heat. Add garlic, almonds and bread and cook for a few minutes until almonds are toasted and the bread lightly fried. Pound to a thick paste, in a mortar or a food processor.

Wipe frying pan with paper towel, and add remaining oil. Add tomatoes, pears, paprika and vinegar, and cook over medium heat, stirring occasionally, for about 10 minutes.

Add the bread and almond paste, saffron (and soaking liquid) and cooked tomatoes to the chickpeas and vegetables. Simmer for a few minutes for flavours to combine and adjust seasoning if needed.

Serve hot, with plenty of fresh bread.

Rabbit & Tomato Stew

Serves 4

about 3 tablespoons
(60 ml/2 fl oz) olive oil

1 × 2-kg (4 lb 6-oz) rabbit,
cut into 8–10 pieces (ask
your butcher to do this)

2 cloves garlic, sliced

1 brown onion, finely chopped

400 g (14 oz) canned crushed
tomatoes

2 sticks celery, finely chopped

2 bay leaves, fresh if possible

1 sprig fresh thyme

1 sprig fresh tarragon

1 cup (250 ml/8½ fl oz) dry
white wine

salt and freshly ground black
pepper

Heat oil in a large, heavy-based non-stick frying pan over medium–high heat. When hot, add rabbit pieces and sauté until lightly browned all over. Remove rabbit from pan and set aside.

Add a little extra oil to the pan if necessary. Add garlic and onion, sauté for 2–3 minutes, then add tomatoes, celery, bay leaves, thyme, tarragon and wine, and stir to combine. Put rabbit pieces back into the sauce, bring to the boil and cook over high heat until liquid reduces by about one-third.

Reduce heat, cover and simmer over very low heat for 1½–2 hours, until meat is very tender and pulls easily away from the bone. Check seasoning. Serve hot, with crusty bread to mop up the sauce.

Basque Fish Stew

Marmitako

Serves 4

3 tablespoons (60 ml/2 fl oz) olive oil

2 cloves garlic, chopped

1 red onion, thinly sliced

500 g (1 lb 2 oz) potatoes, peeled and cubed

400 g (14 oz) canned crushed tomatoes

2 teaspoons Spanish paprika

¾ cup (185 ml/6 fl oz) fish stock

1 bay leaf

400 g (14 oz) canned chickpeas, rinsed and drained

600 g (1 lb 5 oz) skinless tuna or blue-eye fillets, cut into large portions

1 tablespoon finely grated lemon zest

2 tablespoons finely chopped flat-leaf parsley

Heat oil in a heavy-based saucepan over medium heat. Add garlic and onion and sauté for 4–5 minutes, until softened and starting to caramelise. Add potatoes, tomatoes, paprika, stock and bay leaf. Cover and simmer for 15 minutes, until potatoes are cooked.

Add chickpeas and stir. Then add fish, bring to simmering point, reduce heat, cover and simmer for 10–12 minutes, until fish is cooked through. Remove bay leaf, check seasoning and add salt and pepper to taste.

Mix lemon zest and parsley together, sprinkle over stew and serve immediately.

Seafood

Spain's lengthy coastline provides an abundance of seafood. A fresh, local catch is often simply grilled or pan-fried, especially when served as tapas. That said, you will also find seafood poached in wine, crumbed and golden-fried, in fragrant soups and stews, pickled and cured; salt cod (bacalao) is ubiquitous and served in myriad ways.

You will also find seafood recipes in the Tapas and Soups & Stews sections.

< Paprika Prawns with Avocado Salsa (page 86)

Paprika Prawns
with Avocado Salsa

Serves 4

90 g (3 oz) butter, melted

3 tablespoons (60 ml/2 fl oz) olive oil

1 teaspoon salt

freshly ground black pepper

1 tablespoon sweet Spanish paprika

2 teaspoons ground cumin

1 kg (2 lb 3 oz) raw (green) prawns

AVOCADO SALSA

1 small red onion, halved and thinly sliced

2 cloves garlic, sliced

1 avocado, peeled and cubed

2 tablespoons (40 ml/1½ fl oz) extra-virgin olive oil

juice of 1 lemon

1 tablespoon sweet Spanish paprika

Place butter, oil, salt, pepper, paprika and cumin in a large bowl and mix well. Shell and devein the prawns, leaving tails intact. Add prawns to the bowl, stir to coat and then set aside.

To make salsa, put onion, garlic and avocado in a small bowl. Whisk oil, lemon juice and paprika together, pour over the avocado and stir gently to coat. Cover and refrigerate while prawns are cooking.

Preheat the oven grill or barbecue to hot. Cook prawns for 4–5 minutes, turning once or twice and brushing with marinade, until flesh turns pink and opaque. Serve immediately with avocado salsa.

Garlic Prawns

Gambas al ajillo

Serves 4

**250 g (9 oz) small raw (green)
prawns**

**3 tablespoons (60 ml/2 fl oz)
olive oil**

2 cloves garlic, finely sliced

**2 small dried red chillies,
crushed**

salt

Shell and devein the prawns, leaving the tails intact. Pat dry with paper towel.

Heat the oil in a medium-sized non-stick frying pan, or one or more *cazuelas* (see page 9). Add garlic, chillies and prawns and cook over medium–high heat for about 3 minutes, until prawns are opaque and spices are crisp. Sprinkle with salt and serve immediately, with bread to mop up any juices.

✕ If you prefer to cook the prawns in a pan, transfer them to a warmed *cazuela* to serve.

Mussels in White Wine

Serves 4

¼ cup (60 ml/2 fl oz) olive oil

1 onion, finely chopped

2 cloves garlic, chopped

2 large, vine-ripened tomatoes, peeled and chopped

2 cups (500 ml/17 fl oz) dry white wine

1.5 kg (3 lb 5 oz) mussels, scrubbed and debearded

60 g (2 oz) unsalted butter

freshly ground black pepper

2 tablespoons finely sliced spring onions (optional)

Heat the oil in a large, deep saucepan over medium heat. Add onion and garlic and sauté for 3–4 minutes, then add the tomatoes and cook for a further 5–6 minutes, until softened.

Now add the white wine to the pan, bring to the boil, then add the mussels. Reduce heat, cover, and steam for 5–6 minutes, shaking the pan a little, until mussels have opened. Discard any mussels that do not open.

Transfer cooked mussels with a slotted spoon to a warmed bowl. Strain the cooking liquid, then return it to the pan. Add butter and pepper, bring to the boil, stir in spring onions (if using) and simmer for 1 minute. Spoon sauce over the mussels and serve with lots of good bread.

Baby Squid on the Grill

Calamares a la plancha

Serves 4

500 g (1 lb 2 oz) baby squid
tubes

2 tablespoons (40 ml/1½ fl oz)
olive oil, plus extra for
grilling

3 tablespoons (60 ml/2 fl oz)
freshly squeezed lemon juice

grated zest of 1 lemon

2 cloves garlic, crushed

⅓ cup finely chopped flat-leaf
parsley, plus extra to serve

salt and freshly ground
pepper

lemon wedges, to serve
(optional)

Cut the squid tubes open, rinse, and pat dry. Slice into large pieces.

Put olive oil, lemon juice, lemon zest, garlic and parsley in a non-metal bowl
and mix. Add squid, season with salt and pepper and stir to coat. Cover
with cling wrap and refrigerate for at least 30 minutes.

Preheat grill to high, or brush a griddle pan with olive oil and place over high
heat. Add squid pieces and cook for 1–2 minutes, turning once, until just
cooked. Serve immediately, with extra parsley and lemon if desired.

✗ It is important to cook the squid very quickly, or it will become tough.
This form of cooking, traditionally on a very hot metal plate (*plancha*),
is used for many types of seafood, as well as meats.

Galician-style Octopus

Pulpo Gallego

Serves 4

tentacles from 2 octopus, about
  1 kg (2 lb 4 oz), cleaned

2 cloves garlic, sliced

½ onion

6 peppercorns, roughly
  crushed

1 bay leaf

1 teaspoon salt

½ cup (125 ml/4 fl oz) freshly
  squeezed lemon juice

6 tablespoons (120 ml 4 fl oz)
  extra-virgin olive oil

salt and freshly ground black
  pepper

Put octopus tentacles in a large saucepan, cover with cold water, and add garlic, onion, peppercorns, bay leaf, salt and half the lemon juice. Bring to the boil, then reduce heat, cover and simmer for 45–60 minutes, or until tender.

Drain and rinse under cold water. Cut away any dark skin, then slice into bite-sized pieces.

Whisk remaining lemon juice with the oil and season with salt and pepper. Pour this dressing over the octopus and leave to marinate for at least two hours before serving. Serve at room temperature.

✕ This semi-pickle will keep, covered, in the refrigerator for up to 1 week.

Whitebait with Saffron Alioli

Serves 4

a few saffron threads,
  crumbled

1 cup alioli (page 238)

400 g (14 oz) whitebait,
  patted dry

cornflour for dusting

olive oil for deep-frying

salt

Soak saffron in a little warm water for 10 minutes. Mix this liquid with the alioli, cover and refrigerate for 1–2 hours to allow flavour to develop.

Dip whitebait into cornflour and shake off any excess.

Pour about 5 cm (2 in) oil into a large, heavy-based saucepan over medium–high heat. When the oil is hot, cook whitebait in small batches until golden and crisp (about 5 minutes). Remove with a slotted spoon, drain on paper towel, season with a little salt and serve immediately with the saffron alioli.

Sardines Chargrilled in Vine Leaves

Serves 4

12 vine leaves preserved
  in brine
12 fresh sardines, cleaned but
  heads and tails left intact
salt and freshly ground black
  pepper
¼ cup (60 ml/2 fl oz) olive oil
lemon wedges, to serve

Rinse vine leaves and pat dry with paper towel.

Wipe sardines and pat dry with paper towel. Sprinkle with salt and pepper, then wrap each sardine in a vine leaf, leaving head and tail exposed. Brush with oil.

Preheat oven grill or barbecue to high. Chargrill sardine parcels for about 5 minutes, turning once, until cooked.

Serve immediately with lemon wedges.

※ A scoop of garlicky alioli (page 238) goes well with this dish and, of course, some fresh, crusty bread. Preserved vine leaves are sold in jars and are available at most supermarkets and delis.

Prawn Fritters

Serves 4–6

1½ cups (225 g/8 oz) chickpea (besan) flour

½ teaspoon sweet Spanish paprika

salt

2 spring onions, finely chopped

1 tablespoon chopped flat-leaf parsley

250 g (9 oz) freshly cooked prawns, shelled, deveined and roughly chopped

olive oil for deep-frying

lemon wedges and extra paprika, to serve

Put flour, paprika, a good pinch of salt, spring onions, parsley and 1 cup (250 ml/8½ fl oz) water in a bowl and mix to form a batter. Cover and refrigerate for 1 hour.

Place prawns in a food processor and pulse until they are roughly minced (they should still have a little texture). Add to batter and mix well.

Pour oil into heavy-based frying pan to a depth of about 2 cm (¾ in) over medium heat. When oil is hot, drop in spoonfuls of the batter to make small fritters. Cook for about 2 minutes, turning once, until golden brown. Only cook a few fritters at a time, as the oil needs to stay hot. Remove fritters from pan with a slotted spoon, drain on paper towel and keep warm until all fritters are cooked. Serve with lemon wedges and an extra sprinkling of paprika.

Crumbed Mussels

Serves 4–6

1.5 kg (3 lb 5 oz) fresh mussels, scrubbed and debearded

2 tablespoons (40 ml/1½ fl oz) olive oil

1 clove garlic, chopped

1 tablespoon (30 g/1 oz) tomato paste

1 tablespoon (20 ml/¾ fl oz) freshly squeezed lemon juice

pinch of hot Spanish paprika

2 tablespoons finely chopped flat-leaf parsley

salt and freshly ground black pepper

1 tablespoon (20 g/¾ oz) butter

1 cup dry breadcrumbs

SAUCE

1½ tablespoons (30 g/1 oz) butter

2 tablespoons (30 g/1 oz) plain flour

3 tablespoons (60 ml/2 fl oz) milk

3 tablespoons (60 ml/2 fl oz) fish stock

Pour 2 cups (500 ml/17 fl oz) water into a large saucepan and bring to the boil over high heat. Add cleaned mussels, cover and cook for 4–5 minutes. Discard any mussels that do not open. Strain liquid from saucepan and reserve about ½ cup.

Remove mussels from their shells (save the shells), and chop the flesh.

Heat 1 tablespoon (20 ml/¾ fl oz) oil in a non-stick frying pan over medium heat, add garlic and cook for 1–2 minutes. Add tomato paste, reserved mussel liquid, lemon juice, paprika and parsley. Cook, stirring, until the mixture just comes to the boil. Add mussel meat, reduce heat and simmer for 2–3 minutes. Season with salt, if needed, and pepper. Spoon mixture into the reserved mussel shells.

Preheat the oven grill to hot.

Meanwhile make the sauce: melt butter in a small saucepan over low heat, add flour and cook, stirring, for 1 minute. Pour in the milk and fish stock, stirring continuously, then reduce heat and simmer for 2–3 minutes until thick and smooth. Season with salt and pepper. Leave to cool a little.

Spoon sauce over mussel mixture in the shells and place on a baking tray.

Melt butter and remaining oil in small frying pan. Add breadcrumbs and fry until crisp, then sprinkle on top of each filled mussel shell. Place the mussels under the grill, until the sauce is bubbling and heated through.

Transfer to a serving platter and serve hot.

Marinated Fish

Escabeche

Serves 4

1 kg (2 lb 3 oz) fresh tuna,
cut into 2-cm (¾-in) slices

½ cup (75 g/2½ oz) plain flour

¾ cup (185 ml/6 fl oz) olive oil

1 onion, thinly sliced

2 red capsicums,
deseeded and thinly sliced

1 clove garlic, crushed

½ cup pitted green olives, sliced

2 tablespoons baby capers,
drained

½ teaspoon sweet Spanish
paprika

2 tablespoons finely chopped
flat-leaf parsley

½ cup (125 ml/4 fl oz) sherry
vinegar

1 teaspoon salt

freshly ground black pepper

extra chopped parsley, to serve
(optional)

Lightly dust tuna slices with flour and shake off any excess.

Heat 3 tablespoons (60 ml/2 fl oz) of the oil in a large frying pan over medium–high heat. Add half the fish pieces and sauté for about 4 minutes, turning once, until lightly browned. Drain on paper towel. Cook and drain remaining tuna, then set aside.

Add a little extra oil to the frying pan if needed. Sauté onion and capsicum over medium heat for 7–8 minutes, until soft and just starting to brown. Add garlic, olives, capers, paprika, parsley, vinegar, salt and pepper, and stir to combine.

Put a layer of tuna in a shallow ceramic or glass casserole dish. Top with a layer of onion mixture, then repeat layers (ending with the onion mixture). Drizzle with any remaining oil. Cover and refrigerate for at least 8 hours.

Serve scattered with chopped parsley.

Tuna Toasts

Tostados de atun

Serves 4–6

4 slices sourdough bread,
   crusts removed

100 g (3½ oz) canned tuna
   in brine, drained

3 tablespoons (75 g/2½ oz)
   good-quality mayonnaise

1 tablespoon baby capers,
   drained

freshly ground black pepper

sweet Spanish paprika,
   to serve

Toast bread, then cut each slice into strips 3 cm (1¼ in) wide.

Place tuna in a bowl and mash well. Stir through the mayonnaise and capers and season with a good twist of black pepper.

Spread tuna mix over the toast, sprinkle with paprika and serve immediately.

Monkfish with Saffron & Almonds

Serves 4–6

1 kg (2 lb 3 oz) skinless
monkfish fillets, cut into
even-sized pieces

2 tablespoons (40 ml/1½ fl oz)
olive oil

2 cloves garlic, crushed

3 red capsicums, deseeded and
cut into strips

1 cup (250 ml/8½ fl oz) fish
stock

¾ cup blanched almonds,
toasted and finely ground

½ teaspoon saffron threads,
crumbled

½ teaspoon salt

freshly ground black pepper

Preheat oven to 180°C (360°F). Lightly oil a lidded baking dish, add fish and season lightly with salt and pepper. Cover, place in preheated oven and bake for 10–15 minutes. Remove from oven and transfer fish pieces to a plate (reserve the juices for sauce).

Heat oil in a heavy-based saucepan over medium heat. Add garlic and capsicum, and sauté for 2–3 minutes until starting to soften. Reduce heat and cook for a further 10 minutes. Add fish juices, stock, ground almonds, saffron, salt and pepper, stir to combine, then simmer for 5 minutes. Pour mixture into a food processor and blend.

Return sauce to the saucepan, add fish fillets, cover and simmer for 5 minutes or until fish is heated through. Serve immediately.

Baby Clams with Chorizo

Serves 4

2 tablespoons (40 ml/1½ fl oz) olive oil

2 cloves garlic, crushed

120 g (4 oz) cured chorizo, diced

800 g (1 lb 12 oz) canned chopped tomatoes

1 fresh red chilli, deseeded and chopped

1 kg (2 lb 3 oz) baby clams, scrubbed

salt

2 tablespoons chopped fresh coriander

Heat oil in a large saucepan over medium heat, add garlic and chorizo and cook for 2–3 minutes until chorizo starts to brown. Add tomatoes and chilli, bring to the boil, then reduce heat and simmer for 15 minutes, until sauce thickens.

Add clams to sauce and cook over low–medium heat, stirring once or twice, for about 5 minutes. Discard any clams whose shells have not opened.

Check for seasoning, adding salt if needed. Serve immediately, sprinkled with the coriander, and offer plenty of fresh bread for mopping up the sauce.

Trout with Jamon

Serves 4–6

4 small trout (about 250 g/9 oz each), cleaned

6 thin slices jamon

freshly ground black pepper

salt

½ cup (75 g/2½ oz) plain flour, for dusting

60 g (2 oz) butter

2 tablespoons (40 ml/1½ fl oz) olive oil

finely chopped flat-leaf parsley for garnish

lemon wedges, to serve

Rinse trout and pat dry, inside and out, with paper towel.

Place one slice of jamon in the cavity of each trout, season with pepper and secure opening with a toothpick. Finely chop the remaining jamon.

Season flour with salt and pepper, then dust the trout lightly with flour and shake off any excess. Heat butter and oil in a large non-stick frying pan over medium heat until sizzling. Add trout (two at a time) and fry for 5–6 minutes on each side. Turn carefully, using a spatula to keep fish from breaking. When cooked, remove to warmed plates.

Add chopped jamon to the pan and sauté over high heat until crisp. Spoon crisped jamon and the pan juices over the trout, scatter with parsley and serve with lemon wedges.

Baked Sardines

Serves 4–6

3 cloves garlic, crushed

1 cup fine dry breadcrumbs

2 tablespoons finely chopped
  flat-leaf parsley

salt and freshly ground black
  pepper

1 kg (2 lb 3 oz) fresh sardines,
  filleted

⅓ cup (80 ml/3 fl oz) olive oil

lemon wedges, to serve

Preheat oven to 180°C (360°F). Lightly oil a baking dish.

Mix garlic, breadcrumbs and parsley in a bowl with some salt and pepper.
Pat sardine fillets dry, brush with oil, then dip into the crumb mix. Lay the
fillets in a single layer in prepared baking dish and cook in preheated oven
for 10–15 minutes.

Serve hot, with lemon wedges.

Scallops in White Wine

Serves 4

20 medium-sized scallops, rinsed and drained

2 tablespoons (40 ml/1½ fl oz) freshly squeezed lemon juice

3 tablespoons (60 ml/2 fl oz) olive oil

1 onion, finely chopped

60 g (2 oz) jamon, chopped

1 cup (250 ml/8½ fl oz) dry white wine

pinch of saffron threads, crumbled

1 teaspoon sweet Spanish paprika

1 tablespoon chopped fresh chives

½ cup dry breadcrumbs

salt and freshly ground black pepper

extra chopped chives, to serve

Preheat oven to 200°C (390°F). Lightly oil a baking dish. Place the scallops in the dish in a single layer, pour the lemon juice over, then cover and refrigerate.

Meanwhile, heat oil in a frying pan over medium heat. Add onion and jamon and sauté for about 10 minutes, until onion is softened. Add wine and saffron, and cook for a further 5 minutes or so, until sauce is reduced. Stir in paprika, chives and breadcrumbs. Season to taste.

While sauce is still warm, spoon over the scallops. Place in preheated oven and bake for about 5 minutes until golden. Scatter with extra chives and serve immediately.

Squid with Peas

Serves 4

1 kg (2 lb 3 oz) squid, cleaned

4 tablespoons (80 ml/3 fl oz)
olive oil

4 cloves garlic, sliced

1 kg (2 lb 3 oz) juicy tomatoes,
peeled and roughly chopped

2 tablespoons finely chopped
flat-leaf parsley

½ cup (125 ml/4 fl oz) dry
white wine

350 g (12 oz) peas,
fresh or frozen

salt and freshly ground black
pepper

2 tablespoons chopped fresh
mint leaves, to serve

Cut the squid tubes into 2-cm (¾-in) rings, but leave the tentacles whole
(unless they are very long).

Heat the oil in a large frying pan over medium–high heat. Add garlic and
sauté for 1–2 minutes then add squid and sauté for another 1–2 minutes,
until it has a little colour. Add tomatoes, parsley and white wine, bring to
the boil, reduce heat to very low and simmer, uncovered, for 20 minutes,
stirring occasionally.

Add peas and cook for another 3–5 minutes, until peas are tender and
sauce has thickened. Check seasoning, adding salt and pepper to taste.
Scatter with chopped mint and serve immediately.

Vegetable Dishes
& Salads

Vegetables in Spain are often served before a main meat or seafood dish, but are commonly (especially if jamon, eggs or sausage are added) served as the main course. The Mediterranean staples – tomatoes, capsicums, onions and garlic – fresh and dried beans, and seasonal treats such as wild asparagus, are special favourites. Potatoes are also on every menu and are cooked in all manner of ways; from the popular tapa, *patatas bravas*, to side dishes and tortillas.

Traditionally salads are simple – combinations of sun-ripened tomatoes, cucumber and capsicum, fresh greens, plump olives – all glistening with luscious local extra-virgin olive oil.

< Spicy Chickpeas with Roasted Capsicum (page 114)

Spicy Chickpeas
with Roasted Capsicum

Serves 6

12 thick slices breadstick

¾ cup (180 ml/6 fl oz) olive oil

juice of 1 lemon

2 cloves garlic, crushed

2 teaspoons hot Spanish
paprika

400 g (14 oz) canned chickpeas,
rinsed and drained

4 roasted and marinated
capsicums (page 245),
sliced into strips

salt and freshly ground black
pepper

2 tablespoons chopped fresh
mint

Preheat oven to 150°C (300°F).

Brush bread slices with some of the olive oil, place on baking tray and bake
in preheated oven for 6–8 minutes, until lightly toasted.

Put the remaining oil, the lemon juice, garlic and paprika in a medium-sized
bowl and whisk to combine. Add chickpeas, toss to coat with dressing and
lightly crush the chickpeas to a textured mash. Stir in marinated capsicum
strips and season with salt and pepper.

Pile chickpea mixture on toasted bread, sprinkle with mint, and serve.

Potatoes with Garlic Mayo

Patatas alioli

Serves 4–6

olive oil for frying

6 medium-sized potatoes,
   peeled and cut into bite-sized
   cubes

alioli (page 238)

Heat about 4 cm (1½ in) oil in a deep frying pan or heavy-based sauce-pan over medium–high heat, until hot. When the oil is ready, carefully add potatoes and deep-fry until brown and crisp. Remove with a slotted spoon and drain on paper towel.

Place potatoes in a warmed serving dish, spoon alioli over and serve.

Spicy Potatoes

Patatas bravas

Serves 4–6

6 medium-sized potatoes,
peeled and cut into bite-sized
cubes

3 tablespoons (60 ml/2 fl oz)
olive oil

2 cloves garlic, chopped

1 small onion, finely chopped

400 g (14 oz) can crushed
tomatoes

1 tablespoon hot Spanish
paprika

¼ teaspoon cayenne pepper

1 bay leaf

salt and freshly ground black
pepper

2 tablespoons finely chopped
flat-leaf parsley, to serve

Preheat oven to 220°C (420°F). Line a baking tray with baking paper.

Boil potato cubes until just soft. Drain well. Put potatoes in a single layer
and drizzle with about 2 tablespoons (40 ml/1½ fl oz) of oil and bake for
15–20 minutes, turning once or twice, until quite crisp and golden.

While potatoes are cooking, heat remaining oil in a saucepan over medium
heat. Add garlic and onion and fry for 2–3 minutes until softened. Add
tomatoes, paprika, cayenne and bay leaf and stir. Cover and simmer for
10–15 minutes, until thickened and reduced. Season to taste with salt and
pepper.

Put baked potatoes in a warmed dish. Remove bay leaf from tomato sauce and pour sauce over potatoes.

Scatter parsley on top and serve immediately.

✕ In small quantities, Patatas bravas are a popular tapa. If you prefer you can deep-fry the potatoes instead of baking them (see instructions on page 115).

Stuffed Tomatoes

Tomatoes rellenos

Serves 8

8 medium-sized vine-ripened tomatoes

4 hard-boiled eggs, shelled

½ cup (150 g/5 oz) mayonnaise or alioli (page 238)

½ cup fresh breadcrumbs

salt and freshly ground black pepper

8–10 basil leaves, torn

1 tablespoon toasted pine nuts

2 tablespoons sliced black Spanish olives

Cut a small cross on the bottom of each tomato. Place tomatoes in boiling water for 30 seconds, then remove and plunge them at once into iced water (to stop the cooking). Using a sharp knife, peel away the skin.

Slice the tops off the tomatoes. You can use these as 'lids' or discard if the tomatoes are fairly small. Scoop out tomato flesh, using a teaspoon or melon-baller, and place tomatoes upside down to drain. (Save the tomato flesh and use it later in a sauce or soup.)

Mash the eggs with the mayonnaise, breadcrumbs, salt and pepper. Then stir through the basil leaves, pine nuts and olives. Spoon mixture into the tomato shells, pressing down, to fill the hollows, then put on lids (if using). Serve at room temperature.

Lentils with Mushrooms & Leeks

Serves 4–6

500 g (1 lb 2 oz) dried brown
lentils, rinsed

200 g (7 oz) unsliced bacon,
or a ham hock

2 tablespoons (40 ml/1½ fl oz)
olive oil

1 small onion, chopped

2 medium-sized leeks (white
parts only), finely sliced

250 g (9 oz) button
mushrooms, sliced

2 large vine-ripened tomatoes,
peeled and chopped

sprig of fresh rosemary

salt and freshly ground black
pepper

2 tablespoons (40 ml/1½ fl oz)
anise liqueur (such as Anis
del Mono, or Pernod)

Put the lentils in a large, heavy-based saucepan with the bacon or ham hock and enough water to cover. Bring to the boil, skim the surface if necessary, then reduce heat, cover and simmer for 35–40 minutes until lentils are soft but not mushy. Check occasionally to make sure there is enough water.

When lentils are cooked, drain and remove bacon or hock.

Heat oil in a large, non-stick frying pan over medium heat. Add onion and leeks, and cook, stirring occasionally for 5–6 minutes, until softened. Add mushrooms, tomatoes, and rosemary, and cook for 10 minutes until the vegetables start to soften into a sauce. ➤

Roughly dice the bacon, or, if using a ham hock, scrape any meat from the bone and gently pull apart. Add meat and lentils to the pan, stir, cover and simmer over low heat for a further 10 minutes. Season with salt and pepper, then stir the liqueur through the sauce, and serve.

※ Black pudding (*morcilla*) is often added to this dish. If using, cut about 200 g (7 oz) of the sausage into thick slices and add to the frying pan with the lentils.

Russian Salad

Ensaladilla Rusa

Serves 4

700 g (1 lb 9 oz) small, waxy
   potatoes

2 small carrots, cut in half

250 g (9 oz) peas,
   fresh or frozen

2 hard-boiled eggs,
   shelled and quartered

2 tablespoons finely chopped
   fresh chives

⅔ cup (200 g/7 oz) good-
   quality mayonnaise

salt and freshly ground black
   pepper

Boil the potatoes and carrots until tender, then drain. Allow to cool, then peel and cut into small cubes. Place in a serving bowl.

Boil the peas for a few minutes until cooked. Refresh in iced water (to stop the cooking and retain their bright-green colour), then drain and add to the cooked potatoes. Add the hard-boiled eggs and chives, and then carefully stir the mayonnaise through, until everything is lightly coated. Season with salt and pepper to taste. Cover and refrigerate until ready to serve.

✕ This 'Russian' salad is a popular tapa in Spain. Canned tuna is often added.

Basque-style Eggs

Piperada

Serves 2

2 tablespoons (40 ml/1½ fl oz) olive oil

2 cloves garlic, crushed

½ red onion, thinly sliced

2 red capsicum, deseeded and cut into slices

4 large, vine-ripened tomatoes, peeled and chopped

1 sprig fresh thyme

salt and freshly ground black pepper

4 eggs

1 tablespoon finely chopped flat-leaf parsley

croutons (see note on page 63), to serve

Heat oil in a large lidded non-stick frying pan over medium heat. Add garlic and onion and sauté for 2–3 minutes until softened. Add capsicum and cook for another 2–3 minutes, stirring occasionally. Add tomatoes, thyme, salt and pepper. Stir, cover, reduce heat and simmer for 10 minutes or until tomatoes are cooked.

Break eggs into a bowl, being careful not to break the yolks, then slide gently, one by one, over the tomato mixture. Cover pan again and cook until the egg whites are set but the yolks still a little runny.

When eggs are ready, sprinkle with parsley and croutons, and serve immediately.

Baby Leek Salad

Serves 4

16 baby leeks

3 tablespoons (60 ml/2 fl oz) extra-virgin olive oil

2 tablespoons (40 ml/1½ fl oz) sherry vinegar

1 clove garlic, crushed

salt and freshly ground black pepper

2 hard-boiled eggs, shelled and finely chopped

½ cup walnuts, toasted

1 tablespoon chopped fresh coriander

Trim tops and bottoms of leeks and slit lengthways to the centre. Boil the leeks in a small amount of water for 3–4 minutes. Drain, refresh under cold water and drain again.

To make dressing, whisk oil with vinegar and garlic, then season with salt and pepper.

Arrange leeks on a serving platter and pour the dressing over. Scatter the chopped egg, walnuts and coriander on top and serve at room temperature.

※ If you can't buy baby leeks, use instead the smallest leeks you can find, but trim off the green ends, which can be tough.

Cauliflower with Garlic & Almond Picada

Serves 4

1 small cauliflower,
cut into florets

4 cloves garlic,
roughly chopped

3 tablespoons chopped flat-leaf
parsley

1 teaspoon salt flakes

¼ cup (60 ml/2 fl oz) olive oil

½ cup flaked almonds

2 teaspoons sweet Spanish
paprika

1 tablespoon (20 ml/¾ fl oz)
dry sherry

Cook cauliflower in boiling water for 4–5 minutes until tender. Drain (reserving a few tablespoons of cooking liquid), transfer to a heated serving dish and keep warm.

Pound garlic, parsley and salt in a mortar to form a paste. Stir in a few tablespoons of reserved cooking water and half the oil, and mix well.

Heat remaining oil in a non-stick frying pan over medium heat. Add flaked almonds and stir until they are lightly toasted. Reduce heat, add paprika and sherry, stir, then stir in the garlic paste.

Spoon over the cauliflower and serve immediately.

※ A *picada* is a little like an Italian pesto. This version provides a piquant contrast to the cauliflower.

Spinach with Olives & Pine Nuts

Serves 4

3 tablespoons (60 ml/2 fl oz) olive oil

2 cloves garlic, sliced

2 spring onions, chopped

½ cup sliced black Spanish olives

500 g (1 lb 2 oz) baby spinach leaves, rinsed

¼ cup pine nuts, toasted

freshly ground black pepper

extra-virgin olive oil, to drizzle

Heat oil in a large non-stick frying pan over medium heat, add garlic and spring onions, and sauté for 1–2 minutes until softened. Add olives and stir to heat through. Add spinach leaves and toss for a few minutes until just wilted. Drain off any excess liquid.

Add pine nuts, season with freshly ground pepper, drizzle with a little oil and serve.

Golden Saffron Potatoes

Serves 4

1.3 kg (2 lb 14 oz) medium-sized potatoes, peeled and halved

pinch of saffron threads, crumbled

2 tablespoons (40 ml/⅔ fl oz) olive oil

½ teaspoon ground turmeric

salt and freshly ground black pepper

Preheat oven to 180°C (360°F).

Put potatoes into a large saucepan, cover with cold water, add saffron and bring to the boil over a high heat. Reduce heat and boil for about 10 minutes, until almost tender. Drain well.

Return potatoes to saucepan, add oil and turmeric, and season with salt and pepper. Put lid on pan and toss potatoes to coat and roughen edges.

Tip potatoes onto non-stick baking tray or pan and roast in preheated oven for about 40 minutes, until crisp and golden.

Greens, Valdeon Cheese & Smoked Almonds

Serves 6

1 butter lettuce, leaves torn into bite-sized pieces

2 cups rocket leaves, torn into bite-sized pieces

200 g (7 oz) Valdeon blue cheese (or other crumbly blue cheese)

3 tablespoons (60 ml/2 fl oz) extra-virgin olive oil

2 tablespoons (40 ml/1½ fl oz) sherry vinegar

freshly ground black pepper

90 g (3 oz) smoked almonds, roughly chopped

Put lettuce and rocket into a bowl and crumble cheese on top.

Whisk oil, vinegar and pepper to make a dressing. Pour over salad and toss lightly. Scatter almonds on top and serve immediately.

✕ If Spanish Valdeon cheese is unavailable, try another crumbly blue cheese with 'bite', such as Gorgonzola. Smoked almonds can be found in nut shops and most supermarkets.

Tomato & Cucumber Salad

Pipirrana

Serves 4–6

900 g (2 lb) vine-ripened tomatoes, peeled and chopped

1 red capsicum, deseeded and finely chopped

1 small red onion, finely chopped

2 Lebanese cucumbers, thinly sliced

½ cup pitted black Spanish olives

½ cup (125 ml/4 fl oz) sherry vinaigrette (page 247)

Place vegetables and olives in a bowl and toss lightly. Pour vinaigrette over the salad and toss again to coat. Cover, and refrigerate for an hour before serving.

Serve chilled.

※ This is a popular salad in Andalusia. Chopped hard-boiled eggs and tuna in oil – two favourite Spanish ingredients – are sometimes added. Serve with crusty bread for a casual lunch.

White Anchovy, Fennel & Lemon Salad

Ensalada de boquerones

Serves 6–8

⅓ cup (80 ml/3 fl oz) extra-virgin olive oil

2 tablespoons (40 ml/1½ fl oz) red-wine vinegar

freshly ground black pepper

200 g (7 oz) rocket leaves

2 baby fennel bulbs, sliced as thinly as possible (set aside the leafy fronds for garnish)

1 small red onion, sliced as thinly as possible

2 wedges preserved lemon, skin removed, diced

220 g (8 oz) white anchovies

Whisk oil, vinegar and pepper together, to make the dressing.

Put rocket, fennel, onion and lemon in a serving bowl, pour dressing over and toss to combine. Arrange anchovies on top, then scatter with chopped fennel fronds and serve.

✗ Preserved lemons are available in jars, from specialist food stores and delis. You can replace the white anchovies with flaked, smoked trout.

Asparagus & Orange Salad

Serves 4

225 g (8 oz) asparagus spears

2 oranges

1 butter lettuce

2 vine-ripened tomatoes, peeled and quartered

1½ tablespoons (30 ml/1 fl oz) extra-virgin olive oil

2 teaspoons white-wine vinegar

salt and freshly ground black pepper

1 tablespoon chopped flat-leaf parsley, for garnish

Trim asparagus and cut into 5-cm (2-in) lengths. Bring a small pot of water to the boil and blanch the asparagus for 3–4 minutes, until just tender. Drain. Refresh in iced water to stop the cooking process.

Finely grate the zest of 1 orange. Peel the other orange and pull both apart into segments, removing all pith and membrane.

Place lettuce leaves, tomatoes, orange segments and drained asparagus in a salad bowl.

Whisk oil, vinegar and orange zest together to make a dressing, seasoning with salt and pepper. Pour dressing over salad and scatter parsley on top. Toss gently and serve immediately.

Slow-roasted Baby Beets with Goat's Curd & Hazelnuts

Serves 4

- 3 tablespoons (60 ml/2 fl oz) extra-virgin olive oil
- 1 tablespoon (20 ml/¾ fl oz) red-wine vinegar
- salt and freshly ground black pepper
- 2 bunches baby beetroot, scrubbed and trimmed

- 375 g (13 oz) goat's curd or soft goat's cheese
- ½ cup hazelnuts, roasted and chopped
- ½ handful of fresh mint leaves
- extra-virgin olive oil, to drizzle

Preheat oven to 160°C (320°F).

Whisk oil and vinegar together and season with salt and pepper. Set aside.

Lay half of the baby beetroot in a single layer on aluminium foil, then fold foil over to seal. Do the same with the remaining beets. Place both parcels in a baking dish and bake in preheated oven for 30–40 minutes, until tender when pierced with tip of a small knife.

When beetroot are cooked, allow to cool a little, then rub off the skins. **>**

Arrange on a serving platter or individual plates and sprinkle with bits of goat's curd. Pour a little of the dressing over and scatter the hazelnuts on top.

Sprinkle with fresh mint leaves and an extra drizzle of olive oil, and serve.

※ Use rubber gloves when rubbing off beetroot skins otherwise your fingers will be stained pink.

Onion & Orange Salad

Serves 6

2 tablespoons raisins

3 oranges, peeled

1 small red onion, thinly sliced

12 pitted black olives, sliced

⅓ cup (80 ml/3 fl oz) extra-virgin olive oil

1 teaspoon Dijon mustard

2 tablespoons (40 ml/1½ fl oz) lemon juice

salt and freshly ground black pepper

2 tablespoons flaked almonds, lightly toasted

a few torn mint leaves, for garnish

Put raisins in a small bowl or cup, cover with boiling water and soak for 20 minutes. Drain.

Use a sharp knife to cut oranges into segments, making sure to remove all the pith and membrane. Arrange orange segments on a platter and scatter onion, olives and raisins on top.

Whisk together oil, mustard and lemon juice, and season with salt and pepper. Pour dressing over the salad and toss gently. Sprinkle toasted almonds and mint on top, cover, and refrigerate for 1 hour before serving. Serve chilled.

✕ Buy good-quality black olives and slice them yourself – many ready-sliced olives are lacking in flavour.

Chargrilled Catalan Salad

Escalivada

Serves 4

4 small eggplants, halved

1 red onion, halved

4 red capsicums, deseeded and
  then halved lengthways

2 large vine-ripened tomatoes,
  halved

about ½ cup (125 ml/4 fl oz)
  olive oil

2 tablespoons (40 ml/1½ fl oz)
  freshly squeezed lemon juice

2 cloves garlic, crushed

salt and freshly ground black
  pepper

Preheat grill to hot.

Brush vegetables with some of the oil and grill for 15–20 minutes until
they are soft and the edges blackened (some will cook more quickly than
others). Remove vegetables from the grill and allow to cool.

Slice capsicum into strips. Remove ends from eggplant and cut flesh into
strips. Cut tomatoes into quarters and remove cores. Cut onion into thick
slices. Arrange all the vegetables on a serving dish.

To make dressing, whisk remaining oil with the lemon juice and garlic,
then season with salt and pepper. Pour over vegetables and toss gently to
combine.

Serve at room temperature.

Green Beans with Almonds & Cumin

Serves 4

450 g (1 lb) green beans, topped and tailed

2 tablespoons (40 ml/1½ fl oz) extra-virgin olive oil

30 g (1 oz) flaked almonds

1 teaspoon cumin seeds

1 teaspoon hot Spanish paprika

extra olive oil, to serve

salt flakes

Bring a small pot of water to the boil. Blanch the beans for 4–5 minutes, until just soft but still green. Drain.

Heat oil in a frying pan over medium–high heat. Fry almonds for about 30 seconds, then add cumin seeds and fry for a few seconds more. Remove from heat and stir in paprika.

Add cooked beans to the pan, toss to combine. Drizzle with a little extra olive oil, add salt to taste, and serve.

Castilian Red Cabbage

Serves 4–6

800 g (1 lb 12 oz) red cabbage
(about 1 whole cabbage),
finely shredded

2 tablespoons (40 ml/1½ fl oz)
olive oil

3 cloves garlic, sliced

1 small cured chorizo (about
50 g/1¾ oz), cut into small
cubes

100 g (3½ oz) salted pork belly,
chopped into small cubes

2 tablespoons (40 ml/1½ fl oz)
red-wine vinegar

Put shredded cabbage in a large saucepan, pour over enough boiling water to almost cover, then cook over medium heat for about 10 minutes until cabbage has softened. Drain well.

Heat oil in a non-stick frying pan over medium heat. Add garlic, chorizo and pork, and sauté for about 5 minutes, until meat is starting to brown. Add cabbage and stir to combine. Reduce heat and simmer for 15 minutes, stirring occasionally, until cabbage is soft. Stir in vinegar and cook for another 5 minutes.

Serve immediately.

※ Ask your butcher or deli for salted pork belly. If it's not available, pancetta is an acceptable substitute.

Paellas & Other Plates to Share

Large meals in Spain tend to be hearty and substantial – often based around meat and potatoes, legumes or rice – with many regional specialties incorporating ingredients and influences unique to the area. While many non-Spaniards think of paella as emblematic of Spanish food, it is, in fact a regional speciality specific to Valencia. *Cocido Mardrileno* (page 172) – a robust, chickpea-based hotpot – is more widely considered one of Spain's national dishes.

In Spain, paella is not often cooked at home – it is a dish cooked for festive occasions, or at restaurants. Home stoves cannot usually provide enough heat for the wide pan, so finishing off the dish in the oven ensures the rice is cooked through. As with risotto, paella rice should be a little firm when cooked; unlike a risotto, paella should be stirred as little as possible. The best paellas form a delicious crust (*socarrat*) on the underside.

< Paella with Red Capsicum (page 148)

Paella with Red Capsicum

Serves 4

3 tablespoons (60 ml/2 fl oz) olive oil

1 onion, chopped

3 cloves garlic, chopped

2 red capsicums, deseeded and sliced

4 large, vine-ripened tomatoes, peeled and chopped

350 g (12 oz) short-grain paella or risotto rice

4 cups (1 litre/34 fl oz) hot chicken or fish stock

350 g (12 oz) raw (green) prawns, shelled and deveined

225 g (8 oz) peas, fresh or frozen

a few threads of saffron, crumbled

½ teaspoon hot Spanish paprika

sprig of fresh rosemary

salt and freshly ground black pepper to taste

lemon wedges, to serve

alioli (page 238), to serve (optional)

Heat oil in a paella pan or a large, wide frying pan. Add onion and garlic and cook for 5 minutes, stirring, over low heat until onions start to caramelise. Add capsicum and cook for 1–2 minutes. Add tomatoes and cook for about 15 minutes over low heat, stirring occasionally, until the tomatoes thicken to form a sauce.

Add rice to pan, stir to coat in the sauce, and cook for 5 minutes. Now slowly add the hot stock, along with the prawns, peas, saffron, paprika, rosemary, salt and pepper. Stir once, bring to the boil, then cover and simmer over low heat for about 15–20 minutes until stock is absorbed, stirring the dish as little as possible. If there is too much liquid near the end of the cooking time, increase heat to boil it away.

When rice is cooked, turn off heat, cover pan with clean tea towel and leave for 5 minutes.

Serve with lemon wedges and a bowl of alioli on the side, if desired.

✕ Calasparra and Bomba are the best-known Spanish rice varieties for paella, but if they are not available choose a good-quality short-grain rice, such as arborio.

Paella with Chicken & Rabbit

Paella a la Valenciana

Serves 6–8

2 cups (500 ml/17 fl oz) chicken or veal stock

2 sprigs each of fresh thyme and rosemary

a few saffron threads, crumbled

750 g (1 lb 10 oz) chicken legs and thighs

750 g (1 lb 10 oz) rabbit pieces

salt and freshly ground black pepper

5 tablespoons (100 ml/3½ fl oz) olive oil

1 green capsicum, deseeded and finely chopped

1 brown onion, finely chopped

6 cloves garlic, crushed

225 g (8 oz) green beans, halved

2 vine-ripened tomatoes, peeled and chopped

225 g (8 oz) peas, fresh or frozen

3 tablespoons chopped flat-leaf parsley

2 teaspoons sweet Spanish paprika

3 cups short-grain paella or risotto rice

extra chopped flat-leaf parsley and lemon wedges, to serve

Put stock, 4 cups (1 litre/34 fl oz) water, herb sprigs and saffron in a small saucepan and simmer over low heat for 20 minutes to infuse.

Debone chicken and rabbit and cut into bite-sized pieces. Season with salt and pepper.

Preheat oven to 210°C (410°F).

In a paella pan or ovenproof frying pan approximately 45 cm (18 in) wide, heat 3 tablespoons (60 ml/2 fl oz) of the oil over medium–high heat. Sauté chicken and rabbit pieces in batches for about 5 minutes, until lightly browned but not cooked through. Set aside.

Add capsicum, onion and garlic, and sauté until starting to soften. Add beans, and tomatoes and cook for about 2 minutes more, then stir in the peas, parsley and paprika. Add rice and stir to coat, return chicken and rabbit to the pan and strain in the hot stock. Bring to the boil, cook for 5 minutes without stirring, then reduce heat and cook for a few more minutes until most, but not all, of the liquid is absorbed. Check the meat is cooked, and add extra seasoning if needed.

Place pan in preheated oven and cook, uncovered, for 10–12 minutes until rice is cooked. Remove from oven, cover pan with a clean tea towel and leave for 5–10 minutes to absorb any extra moisture.

Scatter with chopped parsley and serve direct from the pan, with lemon wedges on the side.

Seafood Paella

Paella a la marinera

Serves 6–8

24 small mussels, scrubbed and debearded

a few threads of saffron

700 g (1 lb 9 oz) fillets firm, white-fleshed fish (use at least 2 varieties)

450 g (1 lb) small or baby squid with tentacles, cleaned

18 large raw (green) prawns, unshelled

sea salt

6 cloves garlic, crushed

1 tablespoon chopped fresh thyme

2 tablespoons chopped flat-leaf parsley

2 teaspoons sweet Spanish paprika

2 pinches ground cayenne pepper

6 cups (1.5 litres/51 fl oz) fish stock

12 tablespoons (240 ml/ 8 fl oz) olive oil

1 red onion, chopped

2 red capsicums, deseeded and finely chopped

2 vine-ripened tomatoes, peeled and chopped

3 cups short-grain paella or risotto rice

lemon wedges, to serve

aioli (page 238), to serve (optional)

Put 2 cups (500ml/ 17 fl oz) water in a large saucepan, add mussels, bring to the boil, cover and steam for about 5 minutes or until shells open. (Discard any mussels that did not open.) Remove the meat from half the mussels but keep the other half in shells. **>**

Crumble saffron into a little warm water and leave to soak for about 5 minutes.

Cut fish fillets into 2-cm (½-in) cubes. Cut squid into squares, but leave tentacles whole. Place fish, squid and prawns in a bowl, sprinkle with sea salt and leave for 15 minutes.

Put garlic, thyme, parsley, paprika, cayenne and a few drops of water in a mortar and pound to make a paste. Add a little more water or some olive oil if the mixture is very dry.

Heat stock, saffron and its soaking liquid in a saucepan over a medium heat. Cover and keep hot.

Preheat oven to 210°C (410°F).

In a paella pan or ovenproof frying pan approximately 45-cm (18-in) in diameter, heat 6 tablespoons (120 m/4 fl oz) olive oil over medium heat. Add fish, squid and prawns in batches and sauté until they have a little colour, but are not fully cooked. Transfer to a warmed plate.

Add remaining oil, onion and capsicum to the pan and cook gently for 6–7 minutes until vegetables are softening and the onion is starting to caramelise. Increase heat, add chopped tomatoes and cook for a few minutes until they start to soften.

Add rice to pan and stir to coat. Pour in hot stock, bring mixture to the boil and cook for 5 minutes, without stirring. Add fish, squid and garlic paste and gently stir through. Continue to cook for a few minutes until most of the stock is absorbed. If the pan is larger than your burner, move the pan to distribute the heat so all the rice cooks (a heat diffuser is helpful). Check seasoning and add salt if needed.

Add mussel meat to rice, and arrange prawns and mussels in shells on top of rice. Place pan in preheated oven and cook for 8–10 minutes until rice and prawns are cooked (they will turn pink and opaque) and all liquid is absorbed.

Remove pan from oven. Cover with a clean tea towel and leave to rest for 5–10 minutes, to absorb any extra moisture.

Serve paella direct from the pan, with lemon wedges. (Provide bowls for the prawn and mussel shells.)

※ Fish suitable for this paella include snapper, blue eye, bream and mullet.

Spanish Omelette

Tortilla Espagnola

Serves 6

4 medium-sized potatoes,
  peeled and halved

salt

⅓ cup (80 ml/3 fl oz) olive oil

3 cloves garlic, crushed

1 red onion, thinly sliced

6 large eggs

freshly ground black pepper

finely chopped flat-leaf parsley
  and sweet Spanish paprika
  for garnish

Boil potatoes in salted water for 6–7 minutes until half cooked. Drain and cut into thick slices.

Heat oil in a large, heavy-based, non-stick frying pan over medium heat. When it is hot, add garlic and onion and fry for 2–3 minutes. Add potatoes and cook over low heat until potatoes are cooked through (but don't let them colour).

Whisk eggs lightly and season well with salt and pepper. Pour egg mixture over potatoes in the frying pan and tip pan to make sure potatoes are well coated. Cover pan, and cook over low heat for 5–10 minutes until eggs are set. If you like the top to be browned, place until a hot grill for just a minute or so, or slide tortilla onto a plate and then back into the pan to cook the other side.

Slide cooked tortilla onto a large plate, or serve direct from the pan, warm or cold, scattered with parsley and a sprinkle of paprika.

To serve as a tapa, cut into triangles or small squares.

※ In Spain, the potatoes are usually cooked in a very large quantity of oil until soft, which makes for a very rich tortilla. Par-boiling them first reduces the amount of oil needed and produces a lighter dish.

Chorizo Omelette

Tortilla al chorizo

Serves 6–8

⅓ cup (80 ml/3 fl oz) olive oil

200 g (7 oz) cured chorizo, thinly sliced

1 red onion, thinly sliced

600 g (1 lb 5 oz) potatoes, very thinly sliced

6 eggs

1 cup grated manchego cheese (or other firm sheep's cheese)

salt and freshly ground black pepper

2 tablespoons chopped coriander

Heat 1 tablespoon (20 ml/¾ fl oz) of the olive oil in a non-stick frying pan over medium heat, then add chorizo and fry for a few minutes until lightly browned. Remove from the pan and set aside.

Heat a little more oil in the same pan and cook onion and potatoes, stirring, for 3–4 minutes. Reduce heat to low, cover and cook for 20 minutes, checking occasionally, until vegetables are softened.

In a bowl, whisk eggs with the grated cheese and season well with salt and pepper. Stir coriander and cooked chorizo into the eggs, add onions and potatoes, and mix carefully.

Wipe pan, then heat remaining oil. Pour in egg mixture and cook over low heat until almost set, then place it under a hot grill to colour the top. Serve hot or at room temperature.

Spanish Meatballs

Albondigas

Makes about 30

300 g (10½ oz) beef or pork mince

½ cup dry breadcrumbs

1 teaspoon each ground cumin, coriander and nutmeg

3 cloves garlic

salt and freshly ground black pepper

5 tablespoons (100 ml/3½ fl oz) olive oil

1 red onion, finely chopped

1 × 400-g (14-oz) can crushed tomatoes

½ teaspoon sweet Spanish paprika

plain flour, for dusting

1 tablespoon chopped flat-leaf parsley, to serve

Place the mince, breadcrumbs and spices in a bowl, crush 2 cloves of the garlic, add to the mince and mix well. Season with salt and pepper, then refrigerate for an hour for flavours to develop.

Heat 3 tablespoons (60 ml/2 fl oz) of the oil in a large non-stick frying pan or wide saucepan. Chop remaining garlic, add to pan with onion, and sauté for a few minutes, stirring occasionally. Add tomatoes, paprika, and salt to taste, then simmer (uncovered) for 10 minutes until sauce thickens. >

Remove mince from the refrigerator and roll into small balls. Dip into flour to dust lightly.

Heat remaining oil in a separate non-stick frying pan over medium heat. Fry meatballs for about 5 minutes, turning once or twice, until browned all over. Remove from pan, add to the sauce and simmer over medium heat for a further 6–8 minutes (don't let the mixture boil). Stir through chopped parsley and serve.

Roast Pork Loin
with Pedro Ximenez

Serves 4

1 teaspoon sweet Spanish
    paprika

1 kg (2 lb 3 oz) pork loin,
    rinsed and patted dry

salt and freshly ground black
    pepper

225 g (8 oz) sliced jamon

2 tablespoons (40 ml/1½ fl oz)
    olive oil

sprig of fresh rosemary

450 g (1 lb) small onions
    or shallots, quartered

½ cup (125 ml/8½ fl oz) Pedro
    Ximenez sherry, plus extra
    for sauce

½ cup (125 ml/8½ fl oz) veal
    or chicken stock

Preheat oven to 180°C (360°F).

Rub paprika over the pork, then season well with salt and pepper. Wrap jamon around pork loin and tie in place with string.

Put oil in a large roasting pan over medium–high heat on top of the stove. When oil is hot, add pork and fry for 5–6 minutes until browned all over. Tuck rosemary sprig into the string. Add onions to the dish and fry until they start to brown. Pour sherry over pork, add stock, place pan in preheated oven and bake for 1 hour, basting the meat several times. **>**

When pork is cooked, remove from the oven, cover to keep it warm and set aside to rest for 5–10 minutes. Meanwhile, place the roasting pan over medium–high heat, add a little extra sherry to the juices and cook for 1 minute.

Remove string, cut pork into generous slices and arrange on a warmed serving platter with the onions. Spoon sauce over, and serve.

✕ If you don't have Pedro Ximenez sherry, use a good-quality sweet, dark sherry.

Salt Cod Baked with Potatoes

Serves 4

500 g (1 lb 2 oz) salt cod,
   soaked (see page 4)

6 tablespoons (120 ml/4 fl oz)
   olive oil

2 onions, thinly sliced

1 clove garlic, crushed

3 large waxy potatoes, boiled,
   peeled and thickly sliced

freshly ground black pepper

½ cup finely chopped flat-leaf
   parsley, to serve

½ cup black olives marinated
   in oil, to serve

Drain the soaked cod, place in a saucepan, cover with fresh water and bring to the boil over medium heat. Reduce heat and simmer gently for 15 minutes, or until tender. Drain, allow to cool, then flake the fish, removing any bones or skin.

Preheat oven to 200°C (390°F). Lightly oil a baking dish.

Heat 2 tablespoons (40 ml/1 ½ fl oz) of the oil in a non-stick frying pan over medium heat. Add onions and sauté for 10–15 minutes, until soft and starting to caramelise. Add garlic and cook for another 2 minutes, then transfer pan contents to a plate and set aside.

While frying pan is still warm, heat half the remaining oil. Add sliced potatoes and sauté for about 5 minutes, turning once or twice, until they are lightly browned. **>**

Oil a baking dish and arrange half the potatoes on the base, top with flaked cod, then half the onions. Scatter with half of the chopped parsley, add a twist of black pepper, then repeat with remaining ingredients. Drizzle remaining oil over the top.

Bake in the preheated oven for 25 minutes. Scatter with the remaining parsley and olives, and serve.

✕ When choosing salt cod, remember that the narrow tail pieces will be saltier and have more bones – choose a middle piece for best results.

Clams in Fresh Tomato Sauce

Serves 4

3 tablespoons (60 ml/2 fl oz) olive oil

1 red onion, finely chopped

4 cloves garlic, chopped

1 kg (2 lb 3 oz) vine-ripened tomatoes, finely chopped

½ cup chopped flat-leaf parsley

1 bay leaf (fresh if possible)

½ cup (125 ml/4 fl oz) dry white wine or dry sherry

1 kg (2 lb 3 oz) small clams, scrubbed

salt and freshly ground black pepper

Heat oil in a large heavy-based frying pan over medium heat. Add onion and garlic, and sauté for 2–3 minutes until softened. Add tomatoes and continue cooking for 5 minutes, stirring occasionally. Add parsley, bay leaf and wine or sherry, and simmer for 10 minutes until liquid has reduced into a sauce.

Add clams and increase heat. Cover and steam for 4–5 minutes, until shells open. (Discard any clams that do not open.)

Check sauce for seasoning and add salt and pepper to taste. Serve immediately.

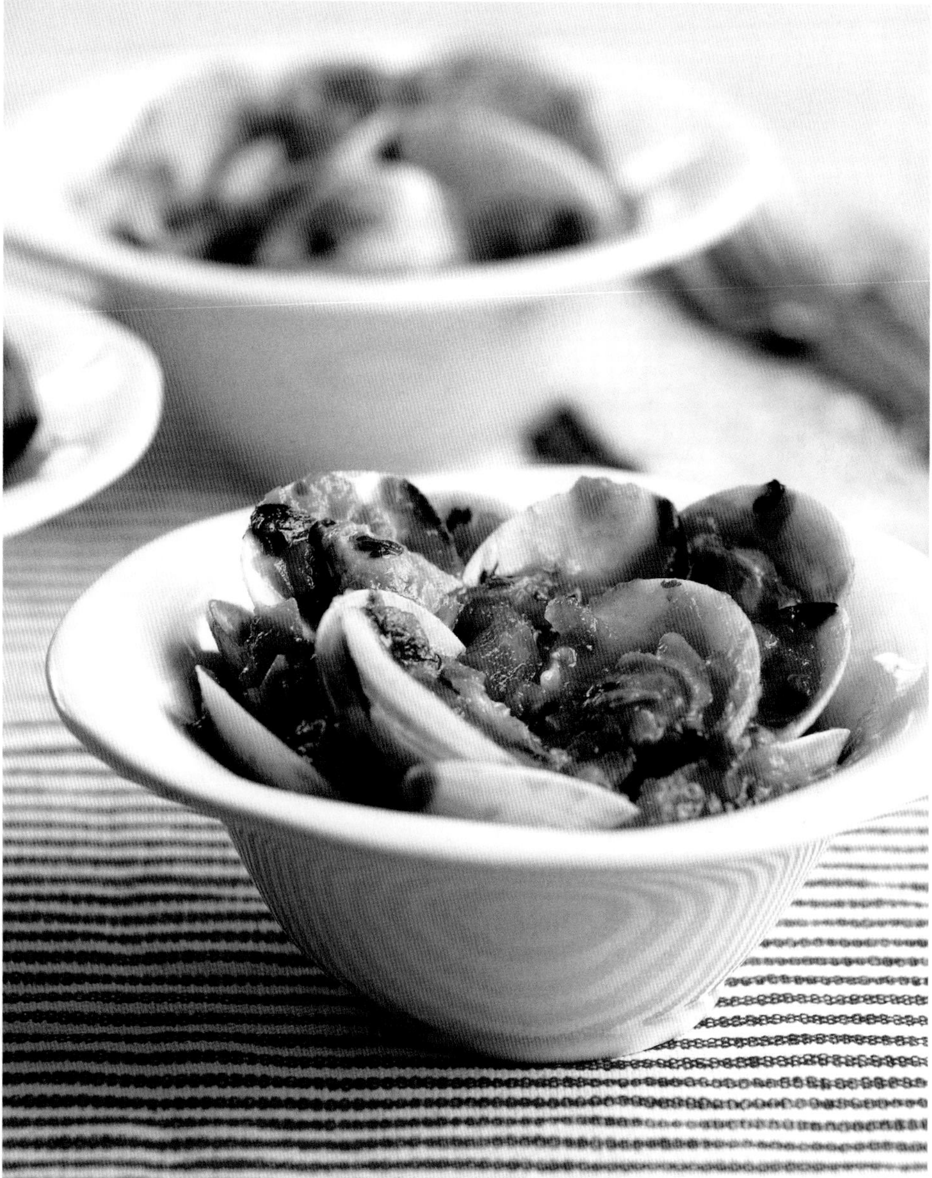

Chickpeas with Tomatoes, Spinach & Almonds

Serves 4

3 tablespoons (60 ml/2 fl oz) olive oil

2 onions, chopped

2 cloves garlic, chopped

400 g (14 fl oz) canned chopped tomatoes

1 cup (250 ml/8½ fl oz) vegetable stock

a few saffron threads, crumbled

1 teaspoon hot Spanish paprika

½ cup flaked almonds, toasted and ground

400 g (14 fl oz) canned chickpeas, rinsed and drained

2 cups chopped baby spinach leaves

salt and freshly ground black pepper

Heat oil in a heavy-based, non-stick saucepan over medium heat. Add onions and garlic, and cook over a low heat, stirring occasionally, for 15–20 minutes until golden and beginning to caramelise.

Add tomatoes to pan and continue cooking for 15 minutes, until mixture becomes a thick sauce. Add stock, saffron, paprika, almonds and chickpeas, and cook for 15 minutes or until most of the liquid has evaporated. Stir chopped spinach through and cook until leaves wilt. Season to taste with salt and pepper. Serve hot or at room temperature.

Madrid Hotpot

Cocido Madrileno

Serves 6

450 g (1 lb) dried chickpeas, soaked overnight

450 g (1 lb) boneless beef shank

1 × 900-g (2-lb) boiling chicken, cut into 8 pieces (see note page 173)

220 g (8 oz) speck (or prosciutto), diced

1 ham bone or bacon hock

5–6 cloves garlic

1 bay leaf

5–6 peppercorns, roughly crushed

3 large carrots, cut into large pieces

2 sticks celery, cut into large pieces

250 g (9 oz) medium-sized potatoes, quartered

225 g (8 oz) fresh chorizo, thickly sliced

salt and freshly ground black pepper

2 cups shredded cabbage

Drain chickpeas, place in a stockpot, add enough cold water to cover by about 5 cm (2 in), and bring to the boil. Skim off any scum.

Add the beef, chicken, speck, ham or bacon bone, garlic, bay leaf and peppercorns. Bring to simmering point, skim off any more scum that rises, cover, and simmer for 1 hour. (Add more water during cooking if needed – the liquid should always cover the ingredients). Now add the carrots, celery, potatoes and chorizo to the pan, and season with salt and pepper. Cover and simmer for another 30 minutes.

When meat and vegetables are tender, stir in shredded cabbage and cook for a few more minutes until it wilts. Serve from the pot or, as is traditional in Spain, serve the broth as the first course, the vegetables as the second course, and the meat as the third course.

✕ If you can't buy a boiling chicken, you can use a roasting chicken. If so, add it after the meat has been simmering for 1 hour.

✕ Different regions have their own version of *cocido*; black pudding (*morcilla*) is a popular addition.

Rabbit with Pancetta & Thyme

Serves 4

750 g (1 lb 10 oz) boned rabbit, cut into 8 even-sized pieces

2 cloves garlic, halved

salt and freshly ground black pepper

8 slices pancetta or thinly sliced bacon

3 tablespoons (60 ml/2 fl oz) olive oil

750 g (1 lb 10 oz) vine-ripened tomatoes, peeled and chopped

2 tablespoons fresh thyme leaves

Preheat oven to 200°C (390°F).

Pat rabbit pieces dry with paper towel. Rub skin with garlic, then season all over with salt and pepper. Wrap a slice of pancetta or bacon around each piece of rabbit.

Heat oil in a medium-sized saucepan, add tomatoes and cook over low heat for 8–10 minutes, until they form a sauce. Stir in thyme, and season with a little salt and pepper.

Spoon tomato sauce over the base of an ovenproof casserole dish. Place rabbit parcels on top, in a single layer. Cover dish, place in preheated oven and bake for 40–50 minutes, basting occasionally, until meat is tender.

Serve hot.

Chicken with Sherry & Garlic

Serves 4

2 tablespoons (40 ml/1½ fl oz) olive oil

1 × 1.8-kg (4-lb) chicken, cut into 8 pieces

salt and freshly ground black pepper

1 tablespoon (20 g/¾ oz) butter

600 g (1 lb 5 oz) chat potatoes, thickly sliced

2 heads of garlic, cloves separated but not peeled

4 sprigs of fresh tarragon

2 bay leaves, fresh if possible

½ cup (125 ml/4 fl oz) medium–dry sherry

Preheat oven to 180°C (360°F).

Heat oil in a wide baking pan over medium heat on top of the stove. Season chicken pieces with salt and pepper, place in pan and cook for a few minutes on each side until golden brown. Transfer chicken to a plate.

Leave baking pan on stove, add butter, then add potato slices, garlic, tarragon and bay leaves, and toss to combine. Return chicken pieces to the dish in a single layer, skin-side up. Pour in sherry and bring to boiling point. Place baking dish in preheated oven and bake, uncovered, for 45–50 minutes, turning once or twice, until chicken is crisp and golden.

Quail Roasted in Vine Leaves

Serves 4

8 quail

salt and freshly ground black
pepper

1 tablespoon grated lemon zest

1–2 tablespoons fresh oregano
leaves

3 tablespoons (60 ml/2 fl oz)
brandy

8 pieces thinly sliced jamon
or bacon, rind removed

about 8 large preserved vine
leaves, rinsed

3 tablespoons (60 ml/2 fl oz)
freshly squeezed lemon juice

Preheat oven to 200°C (390°F). Oil a baking dish that will hold the quail
in one layer.

Rinse quail inside and out, and pat dry. Season cavity with salt and pepper,
lemon zest and oregano, and spoon in a little brandy.

Wrap a piece of bacon around each quail, then wrap in a vine leaf (if vine
leaves aren't large enough, you may need to use extra). Tie a piece of string
around the quail, to secure.

Arrange quail in a single layer in the baking dish and place in preheated
oven for about 15 minutes. To test if they are cooked, insert a skewer into
the flesh – the juices should run clear. **>**

Transfer quail to a warmed serving platter, remove string and keep warm. Pour lemon juice into a saucepan with the pan juices, stir to combine, and heat through.

Spoon sauce over the quail and serve immediately.

✕ If you prefer, you can use jamon or prosciutto instead of bacon.

Oxtail Braised in Red Wine

Serves 4

2.5 kg (5½ lb) oxtail, cut into 5-cm (2-in) lengths (ask the butcher to do this for you)

salt and freshly ground black pepper

plain flour, for dusting

¾ cup (180 ml/6 fl oz) olive oil

2 brown onions, chopped

2 cloves garlic, chopped

2 carrots, chopped

2 sticks celery, chopped

2 tablespoons (50 g/1¾ oz) tomato paste

3 cups (750 ml/25 fl oz) beef or veal stock

2 cups (500 ml/17 fl oz) dry red wine

1 bay leaf

1 sprig of fresh thyme

finely chopped flat-leaf parsley, for garnish

Rinse oxtail in cold water, then pat dry with paper towel. Season with salt and pepper, dip into flour to coat, and shake off any excess.

Heat oil in a wide, heavy-based non-stick saucepan over medium–high heat. Add oxtail pieces in batches, sautéing for 5–6 minutes until lightly browned. As you finish each batch, set aside on a plate. If there is quite a lot of fat in the pan when you have finished, drain this off, leaving just enough to fry the vegetables. **>**

Add onions, garlic, carrot and celery to saucepan and cook, stirring, for 10–12 minutes, until onion is lightly browned and vegetables softening. Return oxtail to the pan, add tomato paste, stock and wine. Stir to combine, then add bay leaf and thyme. Bring to simmering point, cover, reduce heat, and simmer for 2–2½ hours, until oxtail is very tender.

Remove oxtail pieces and place on a warmed serving dish. Remove bay leaf and discard. Purée remaining ingredients in a blender, then strain back into the pan. Check seasoning, reheat sauce and then spoon it over the oxtail. Scatter with parsley and serve hot.

※ Creamy mashed potato is delicious with this, soaking up the rich sauce.

Pork Belly with Thyme & Red Wine

Serves 4–6

salt

1 kg (2 lb 3 oz) pork belly

1 tablespoon (20 ml/¾ fl oz) olive oil

2 sprigs fresh thyme

2 tablespoons cumin seeds

RED-WINE SAUCE

2 tablespoons (40 ml/1½ fl oz) olive oil

1 small red onion, finely chopped

sprig fresh thyme

1 tablespoon (20 ml/¾ fl oz) red-wine vinegar

1 cup (250 ml/8½ fl oz) dry red wine

Press salt onto the pork rind about 1 hour before cooking (this absorbs some of the moisture).

Preheat oven to 220°C (420°F).

Scrape salt off the pork and pat dry with paper towel. Pour oil into an oven-proof dish and put in oven for a minute to heat. When oil is warm, place pork in the dish, rind down. Add thyme sprigs and scatter pork with cumin seeds.

Place pork in preheated oven and roast for 30 minutes. Reduce heat to 190°C (375°F) and roast for another 30 minutes, then turn meat over and roast for 10–15 minutes more. >

To make the sauce, heat oil in a small saucepan over medium heat. Add onion and thyme, and sauté for 2–3 minutes until onion softens. Add vinegar and cook for 1 minute, then add wine and cook over medium–high heat for about 5 minutes until sauce reduces.

Remove pork from oven to a warmed dish, cover to keep warm and leave to rest for at least 5–10 minutes. To serve, slice pork and spoon red-wine sauce over.

Sherry Chicken with Orange

Serves 6

1 tablespoon (20 ml/¾ fl oz) olive oil

6 chicken maryland pieces (about 1.3 kg/3 lb)

1 brown onion, finely chopped

1 medium-sized carrot, finely chopped

1 bay leaf

½ cup (125 ml/4 fl oz) dry sherry

3 teaspoons finely grated orange zest

¾ cup (185 ml/6½ fl oz) freshly squeezed orange juice, strained

1 cup (250 ml/8½ fl oz) chicken stock

1 small orange, peeled, pith removed and lesh cut into cubes

1 cup pimento-stuffed green olives, drained

Preheat oven to 180°C (360°F).

Heat oil in a large, heavy-based frying pan over medium–high heat and sauté chicken in batches, for about 5–6 minutes, until golden brown. Transfer chicken to a large roasting dish.

Pour excess fat from pan, leaving enough to sauté vegetables. Reduce heat, add onion and sauté until softened and starting to brown. Add carrot and bay leaf and cook, stirring occasionally, for about 5 minutes until softened.

Pour in sherry and cook for 1 minute, then add orange zest, juice and stock. Bring to the boil, stir well, and scrape up any bits that have stuck to the bottom of the pan. Pour sauce over the chicken, place dish in preheated oven and bake for about 1 hour, until chicken is cooked.

Remove dish from the oven, pour off juices into a small saucepan, cover chicken and keep warm. Skim any oil from surface of cooking juices, then bring to the boil and simmer for 10 minutes until sauce thickens and reduces.

Pour sauce over chicken, then scatter orange cubes and olives on top. Return chicken to the oven, uncovered, and bake for about 5 minutes, or until orange is warmed through.

Saffron Chicken
with Garlic Picada

Serves 4

1.5 kg (3 lb 5 oz) chicken,
cut into 8 serving pieces

salt

2 teaspoons sweet Spanish
paprika

1 teaspoon saffron threads

½ cup (125 ml/4 fl oz) dry
white wine

4 tablespoons (80 ml/3 fl oz)
olive oil

1 slice good-quality, day-old
white bread, crusts removed,
cut into cubes

8 cloves garlic, lightly smashed

¾ cup (185 ml/6½ fl oz)
chicken or vegetable stock

freshly ground black pepper

Pat chicken pieces dry with paper towel, then rub well with salt and paprika.
Crumble saffron into the white wine and leave to soak.

Heat oil in a large, heavy-based non-stick frying pan over medium heat. Add
bread cubes and fry until golden, then remove from pan and set aside.
Add garlic to pan and sauté for 1–2 minutes, remove and set aside.

Add chicken pieces to pan and cook, turning occasionally, for about
10 minutes, until lightly browned all over. Add saffron-infused wine and
the stock. Cover, reduce heat and simmer over very low heat for about
20 minutes.

Meanwhile, put garlic in a mortar with a little salt and plenty of black pepper, and pound. Gradually add the fried bread and mash everything to a paste (you could do this in a food processor). Add a little liquid from the frying pan to dilute the paste.

When chicken is almost cooked, stir in the garlic paste, and simmer for another 5 minutes until sauce thickens and chicken is cooked. Remove pan from the heat and leave chicken stand for a few minutes before serving.

※ If you prefer, buy chicken pieces on the bone, including some thighs for maximum flavour.

※ A *picada* is a paste added to a dish towards the end of the cooking time, to boost aroma, flavour and texture. The ingredients vary but typically include garlic, oil, herbs, bread (toasted or fried) and nuts. Other flavourings, including herbs, may also be added.

Slow-cooked Lamb with Lemon

Serves 4

1 kg (2 lb 3 oz) boneless lamb
shoulder, cut into bite-sized
cubes

salt and freshly ground black
pepper

2 tablespoons (40 ml/1½ fl oz)
olive oil

1 onion, chopped

3 cloves garlic, crushed

1 tablespoon sweet Spanish
paprika

juice of 1 lemon

1 teaspoon grated lemon zest

½ cup finely chopped flat-leaf
parsley

¾ cup (185 ml/6½ fl oz)
chicken stock

extra chopped flat-leaf parsley
and grated lemon zest,
for garnish

Season lamb with salt and pepper. Heat oil in a heavy-based, non-stick saucepan over medium heat. Add lamb in batches and sauté for 6–8 minutes until browned all over. Transfer cooked meat to a plate.

In the same saucepan, sauté onion and garlic for about 5 minutes until softened. Add paprika, lemon juice and zest, parsley and stock, and stir. Return lamb pieces to the pan and bring to the boil. Reduce heat to very low, cover and simmer for 1–1½ hours, checking occasionally. When lamb is very tender, add salt and pepper to taste. Scatter with extra parsley and lemon zest, and serve hot.

Sweets

The Spanish definitely love their sweets – from crispy *churros* dipped in rich hot chocolate, to milky custards and myriad small cakes and biscuits.

The generous use of almonds and other nuts, plump figs, and spices such as cinnamon, nutmeg and cloves, are a reminder of the influence of the Arab world. The oranges and lemons that thrive in the Mediterranean climate add a citrus tang to many sweet treats.

< Walnut Pastry Puffs (page 194)

Walnut Pastry Puffs

Casadielles

Makes 16

100 g (3½ oz) shelled walnuts, crushed

3 tablespoons (45 g/1¾ oz) caster sugar

2 tablespoons (40 ml/1½ fl oz) anise liqueur (such as Anis del Mono, or sambuca)

30 g (1 oz) butter, melted

4 sheets ready-rolled puff pastry

1 egg white, lightly beaten

icing sugar, for garnish

Preheat oven to 220°C (420°F). Line a baking tray with baking paper.

Put walnuts, sugar, liqueur and melted butter in a small bowl and mix to combine.

Cut pastry into rectangles about 11 cm × 6 cm (4½ in × 2½ in). Put a small spoonful of walnut mixture along the centre of each pastry rectangle. Brush edges with egg white, then fold over pastry, joining long sides first, and press edges to seal. Place on baking tray and bake in preheated oven for 15–20 minutes, until puffed and lightly browned.

Serve warm, dusted with icing sugar.

✕ Typically served at Christmas time in northern Spain, these fragrantly delicious mouthfuls are usually eaten warm. Make sure the walnuts are fresh, as stale ones can be bitter.

Almond & Chocolate Figs

Serves 4

½ cup flaked almonds

30 g (1 oz) good quality dark
  chocolate, chopped

a few drops of amontillado
  sherry

8 firm fresh figs

crème fraîche and cocoa
  powder, to serve (optional)

Place flaked almonds in a non-stick frying pan and cook over medium heat, stirring, for a few minutes, until they are lightly toasted.

Preheat oven to 180°C (360°F). Line a small baking dish with baking paper.

Put toasted almonds, chocolate and sherry into food processor and pulse until mixture has the consistency of breadcrumbs.

Remove stems from figs and cut a cross in the top of each. Push gently to open top of the fig and stuff with chocolate mixture. Gently pinch closed.

Place figs in baking dish and bake in preheated oven for 10–15 minutes until warmed through. Serve warm or at room temperature, with a small scoop of crème fraîche and a dusting of cocoa powder.

✕ If you can find very plump dried figs, you could also use them to make this recipe.

Rice Pudding

Arroz con leche

Serves 4

2 cups (500 ml/17 fl oz) full-cream milk

1 cinnamon stick

1 strip lemon zest, about 5 cm (2 in) long

a few drops of vanilla extract

½ cup short-grain rice

2 egg yolks, lightly beaten

90 g (3 oz) caster sugar

60 g (2 oz) butter

ground cinnamon, to serve

Pour milk into a medium-sized saucepan, add cinnamon stick, lemon zest and vanilla extract, and heat just below boiling point. Strain milk, then return to saucepan. Add rice and egg yolks, and simmer over a medium–low heat for 20 minutes, stirring gently to prevent the mixture sticking.

When rice is completely cooked, stir in caster sugar and butter, and continue cooking for a few minutes.

Serve warm or at room temperature, sprinkled with ground cinnamon.

Figs with Oranges & Walnuts

Serves 6

12 dried figs, stems removed

3 tablespoons (30 g/1 oz) honey

1 teaspoon finely grated lemon zest

1 cinnamon stick

3 oranges, peeled

½ cup walnuts, toasted

natural yoghurt or crème fraîche, to serve

Put figs, ½ cup (120 ml/4 fl oz) water, honey, lemon zest and cinnamon stick in a saucepan. Place over medium heat and simmer gently for 15–20 minutes, stirring occasionally, until figs are soft. Set aside, and discard cinnamon stick.

Remove any pith from the oranges, cut flesh into thin slices and put in a bowl (catch any juice and add to the bowl). Add cooked figs and syrup to the bowl and stir gently to combine. Leave to cool, then chill in refrigerator.

Stir through the toasted walnuts and serve with natural yoghurt or crème fraîche.

Almond Lemon Cake

Serves 8–10

4 eggs

175 g (5½ oz) caster sugar

½ teaspoon ground cardamom

juice and finely grated zest
   of 1 lemon

few drops of vanilla extract

400 g (14 oz) ground almonds

icing sugar, for dusting

crème fraîche,
   to serve (optional)

Preheat oven to 190°C (375°F). Lightly grease a 20-cm (8-in) round cake tin and line base with baking paper.

Beat eggs until light and fluffy. Add sugar a few spoonfuls at a time, beating well after each addition, until mixture is thick and creamy. Fold in cardamom, lemon juice and zest, vanilla extract and ground almonds until mixed (do not beat).

Pour mixture into prepared cake tin. Bake in preheated oven for 35–40 minutes. When cake is ready, it will be coming away from sides of the tin and firm to the touch in the centre. Leave to stand for 10 minutes, then invert onto a cake rack to cool.

Serve dusted with icing sugar, with a dollop of crème fraîche.

Spanish Doughnuts

Churros

Serves 4

100 g (3½ oz) butter
pinch of salt
1 cup (150 g/5 oz) plain flour
3 eggs, lightly beaten

vegetable or olive oil
for deep-frying
caster sugar and ground
cinnamon, for dusting
(optional)

Put 1 cup (250 ml/8½ fl oz) water, butter and salt in a heavy-based saucepan over medium–high heat and bring to the boil. Pour in flour and beat with a wooden spoon until flour is completely mixed and dough forms a ball.

Leave dough to cool a little. Then add the beaten eggs, a little at a time, beating well after each addition, until combined. Spoon mix into a churro-maker or a piping bag with a large fluted nozzle.

Heat 4–5 cm (1½–2 in) of oil in a heavy-based saucepan until very hot (180°C/350°F). To test, drop in a small cube of bread – it should sizzle and turn brown within 15 seconds. Reduce heat, then pipe 10-cm strips (or loops) directly into the oil. (Only cook 3 or 4 churros at a time, to keep the oil hot.) Deep-fry for a minute or so, turning once, until golden. **>**

Remove churros with a slotted spoon or tongs, and drain on paper towel. While still warm, dust with sugar and cinnamon (if using). Serve with warm chocolate sauce (page 203), or hot chocolate for dipping.

✕ Churros are a classic Spanish breakfast treat, but make a delicious snack at any time. Churro-makers (*churreras*), designed for extruding the batter, are available from specialist cookware shops and Spanish food stores.

Chocolate Sauce

Makes about 2½ cups

2 cups (500 ml/17 fl oz) milk

2 teaspoons cornflour

100 g (3½ oz) good-quality
   dark chocolate, chopped

3 tablespoons (45 g/1½ oz)
   caster sugar

pinch of ground cinnamon

Pour about a quarter of the milk into a small bowl, add cornflour and whisk to combine. Set aside.

Pour remaining milk into a medium-sized saucepan over low heat, add chocolate and stir until chocolate has melted. Add milk/cornflour mix, sugar and cinnamon, and continue stirring over low heat for another 5 minutes until mixture thickens.

Serve warm as a dipping sauce for churros (page 201), or with ice-cream.

Catalan Cream

Crema Catalana

Serves 6

1 litre (34 fl oz) full-cream milk
1 vanilla pod, split open
1 tablespoon (15 g/½ oz)
   cornflour

6 egg yolks
200 g (7 oz) caster sugar
extra 4 tablespoons (60 g/2 oz)
   caster sugar, for toffee crust

Put milk in a medium-sized saucepan with vanilla pod over medium heat and bring slowly to the boil. Remove from the heat and leave to infuse for 1 hour, then strain and leave to cool.

Mix cornflour with 3 tablespoons (60 ml/2 fl oz) of the cooled milk. Beat egg yolks with the sugar until pale, then stir in the cornflour mixture. Add the egg mixture to the remaining cooled milk, place over medium heat and cook, stirring, until the custard thickens. Pour into individual ovenproof dishes and refrigerate until ready to serve.

To serve, sprinkle sugar in a thin layer on top of each custard and place under a very hot grill (or use a kitchen blowtorch) until a toffee crust forms.

※ For a modern spin on this creamy dessert, add the finely grated zest of 1 lime to the milk instead of the vanilla pod.

Coffee Liqueur Flan

Serves 6–8

¾ cup (150 g/5 oz) caster sugar

1 × 400-g (14-oz) can
sweetened condensed milk

950 ml (2 pt) full-cream milk

5 eggs

1 tablespoon (20 ml/¾ fl oz)
strong espresso coffee

1 tablespoon (20 ml/¾ fl oz)
coffee liqueur

pinch of salt

double cream,
to serve (optional)

Preheat oven to 180°C (350°F).

Put sugar in a small, heavy-based saucepan over medium heat and leave it, without stirring, until sugar starts to melt. Then stir occasionally until it melts completely and turns a light golden colour. Pour it into a 23-cm (9-in) cake tin and turn tin so caramel covers the base. (Take care, as the caramel is very hot). Allow to set.

Put remaining ingredients in a blender and blend until smooth. Pour mixture through a fine sieve over the caramel base. Cover loosely with aluminium foil. >

Place cake tin in a larger baking pan, at least 5 cm (2 in) deep. Pour boiling water into the outer pan to a depth of about 2.5 cm (1 in), then carefully place pan in preheated oven and bake for 1–1¼ hours. The custard is ready when it is set, but still moves gently, and a knife inserted in the centre comes out clean. Remove from oven and allow to cool completely. Transfer to refrigerator and chill overnight or for at least 8 hours.

To remove flan from tin, run a knife carefully around the edge to loosen. Place a large platter over the tin, then carefully invert, holding dish and plate together. The caramel will form a sauce over the flan.

Serve chilled, with cream if desired.

Seville Oranges with Cinnamon Wine Syrup

Serves 6

3 cups (750 ml/25 fl oz) light
    red wine (tempranillo or
    beaujolais are good)

1 cup (220 g/8 oz) caster sugar

1 cinnamon stick

3 cloves

finely grated zest of ½ orange

6 oranges

Put wine, sugar, cinnamon, cloves and orange zest in a saucepan and stir over medium heat until sugar dissolves. Bring to the boil, and boil uncovered for about 15 minutes until the liquid reduces to a syrup. Allow to cool, then cover and refrigerate. (Syrup can be made a day ahead.)

Peel oranges and remove all pith and membrane. Using a very sharp knife, cut oranges into segments, saving any juice. Divide segments and juice between serving bowls.

Spoon chilled syrup over the fruit, and serve.

Spanish Cakes

Magdalenas

Makes 24

3 cups (450 g/1 lb) plain flour

1 teaspoon baking powder

pinch of salt

1 large egg,
   at room temperature

1¼ cups (275 g/9½ oz) caster
   sugar

1 tablespoon finely grated
   lemon zest

1 cup (250 ml/8½ fl oz) milk

1 cup (250 ml/8½ fl oz) light
   olive oil

icing sugar, for dusting

Preheat oven to 175°C (345°F). Arrange paper patty cases on a tray, or lightly grease a cupcake pan.

Sift flour with baking powder and salt. Beat egg, sugar and lemon zest until pale and fluffy. Gradually fold in milk, oil and sifted flour, mixing well after each addition.

Spoon mixture into cases, filling about two-thirds full. Place in preheated oven and bake for 15 minutes, until puffed and golden.

Transfer to a cake rack to cool. Dust with icing sugar to serve.

Fig Roll

Pan de higo

Serves 8–10

750 g (1 lb 10 oz) dried figs
(stems removed), chopped

½ cup blanched almonds,
toasted and chopped

½ cup hazelnuts,
toasted and chopped

1 tablespoon sesame seeds,
lightly toasted

1½ tablespoons (15 g/½ oz)
icing sugar

1 teaspoon ground cinnamon

¼ teaspoon ground cloves

1 tablespoon (20 ml/¾ fl oz)
brandy

60 g (2 oz) good-quality dark
chocolate, melted

extra icing sugar,
to serve (optional)

Put chopped figs, almonds, hazelnuts, sesame seeds, sugar, cinnamon and cloves in a food processor and process until mixture starts to come together. It will be sticky, but should have some texture.

Tip the mixture into a bowl and stir in brandy and melted chocolate, to form a mixture that is quite stiff and sticky. Add a little more brandy if it is not holding together.

Lay two sheets of aluminium foil or baking paper on the work surface and sprinkle with icing sugar. >

Shape mixture into two small logs and roll up each one tightly in a sheet of the foil or paper. Twist ends to secure. Store in a cool place, or refrigerate, for at least 2 days before serving.

To serve, bring logs back to room temperature and use a sharp knife to cut into slices.

Dust with extra icing sugar if desired.

※ This delectable sweet is perfect served with a strong coffee or an Amontillado sherry, or as part of a cheese platter.

Fried Milk

Leche frita

Serves 6

3 cups (750 ml/25 fl oz) full-cream milk

1 strip lemon zest, 5 cm (2 in) long

1 cinnamon stick

180 g (6½ oz) butter

½ cup (75 g/2½ oz) plain flour

180 g (6½ oz) caster sugar

6 egg yolks

1 egg, whisked

2 cups fine dry breadcrumbs

vegetable oil for deep-frying

icing sugar and ground cinnamon, to serve

Lightly oil a 20-cm (8-in) square baking tin.

Put milk, lemon zest and cinnamon stick in a saucepan over medium–high heat. Bring to the boil, then reduce heat and simmer for 5 minutes. Remove from heat, cover to keep warm and leave to infuse for 5 minutes, then strain. Discard lemon zest and cinnamon stick.

In another saucepan, melt butter over low heat. Add flour and cook, stirring constantly, for 5 minutes. Take pan off the heat, slowly pour in the warm milk, whisking to mix. Add sugar and whisk again, then return to low heat and stir continuously until mixture thickens and coats the spoon. >

Remove mixture from heat and gradually whisk in egg yolks. Return pan to heat and continue stirring until mixture forms a thick custard. Pour the custard into prepared baking pan, smooth the surface, cover, and refrigerate overnight.

When ready to serve, cut the custard into 8 squares, or small triangles if you prefer. Dip custard pieces into egg, then into breadcrumbs, to coat lightly.

Heat about 2.5 cm (1 in) of oil into a large, deep frying pan until hot. Fry custard pieces in batches, turning once, for 3–4 minutes. Drain on paper towel.

Dust with icing sugar and ground cinnamon, and serve warm or at room temperature.

Custard Tarts

Makes 12

225 g (8 oz) caster sugar

1½ tablespoons (25 g/¾ oz)
cornflour

2 cups (500 ml/17 fl oz) milk

½ cup (125 ml/4 fl oz)
thickened cream

3 egg yolks, lightly beaten

3 sheets ready-rolled butter
puff pastry

Place sugar and ½ cup (125 ml/4 fl oz) water in a saucepan over medium–high heat. Cook, stirring, for 2–3 minutes until sugar dissolves. Bring to boil and boil, without stirring, for 3 minutes, to make a syrup. Leave to cool.

Put cornflour in a bowl and gradually add milk, stirring until combined. Add cream and mix well again. Whisk in the egg yolks, then add sugar syrup and whisk again until combined.

Pour mixture into a clean saucepan and cook over medium heat, stirring, until custard comes just to the boil. Remove from heat and set aside to cool.

Preheat oven to 220°C (420°F). Lightly oil a 12-hole, non-stick muffin pan, or 12 individual small tart pans. >

Cut pastry into 12 × 8-cm (3-in) rounds. Press pastry into oiled pans and prick base with a fork. Spoon in the custard, half-filling the pastry cases. Place on top rack of preheated oven and bake for 15–20 minutes until pastry is golden.

Remove tarts from oven, leave to cool in tray for a few minutes, then transfer to a cooling rack.

Serve warm or at room temperature, preferably on the day they are made.

✕ Some dark spots will appear on the pastry and custard as the tarts cook: this is quite traditional.

✕ The custard will sink a little as the tarts cool.

Peaches Poached in Red Wine

Serves 4

4 ripe white peaches

1½ cups (375 ml/12½ fl oz) dry red wine

½ cup (110 g/4 oz) caster sugar

1 cinnamon stick

1 tablespoon freshly squeezed lemon juice

1 teaspoon grated lemon zest

cream or ice-cream, to serve (optional)

Put peaches in a bowl or saucepan, cover with boiling water and leave for 30 seconds. Transfer peaches to a bowl of iced water, leave for another 30 seconds, then remove and peel off skins (they should slip off easily).

Put wine, 1½ cups (375 ml/ 12 ½ fl oz) water, sugar, cinnamon stick, lemon juice and zest in a saucepan and stir to mix. Add peeled peaches in a single layer. Place saucepan over medium heat and bring to a simmer. Cover and simmer for 15 minutes.

Use a slotted spoon to transfer peaches to a serving bowl.

Bring the liquid in the saucepan to the boil and boil for a few minutes until it reduces to a syrup. Pour syrup over peaches and leave to cool. Refrigerate until well chilled.

Serve chilled, with cream or ice-cream.

✕ You can substitute pears for the peaches. Lightly toast a handful of slivered almonds to sprinkle over the fruit before serving.

Almond Biscuits

Polvorones

Makes about 14

120 g (4 oz) blanched
   almonds, lightly toasted
125 g (4½ oz) butter,
   at room temperature
150 g (5 oz) caster sugar

½ teaspoon vanilla extract
generous pinch of ground
   cinnamon
225 g (8 oz) plain flour, sifted
icing sugar, for dusting

Preheat oven to 120°C (250°F). Line a baking tray with baking paper. Put almonds in a blender and process until finely ground.

Beat butter, sugar, vanilla extract and cinnamon together until pale and creamy. Use a spoon to beat in the flour and ground almonds, until soft and crumbly. Take a walnut-sized ball of the mixture and place on the prepared baking tray. Press gently to form small disc about 2 cm (¾ in) thick. Repeat with remaining mixture, leaving plenty of space between each biscuit.

Place in preheated oven and bake for 25 minutes (they should still be quite pale). Allow to cool completely before transferring carefully from the tray: use a spatula, as they break very easily). Dust generously with icing sugar before serving.

✕ A special treat at Christmas time, *polvorones* are traditionally made with lard, but this buttery version has the same delicate, crumbly texture and is just as delicious.

Raspberry & Cava Sorbet

Serves 4

½ cup (110 g/4 oz) caster
  sugar

350 g (12 oz) fresh raspberries,
  rinsed

1 cup (250 ml/8½ fl oz) freshly
  squeezed orange juice

1 cup (250 ml/8½ fl oz) brut
  cava or other dry sparkling
  wine

Stir sugar and 3 tablespoons (60 ml/2 fl oz) water in a small saucepan over medium–low heat until sugar dissolves. Pour syrup into a bowl.

Purée raspberries in a food processor, then strain purée to remove seeds. Add purée to sugar syrup, then stir in orange juice and cava. Cover and refrigerate until chilled.

Pour raspberry mix into an ice-cream maker and follow manufacturer's instructions. When sorbet is ready, transfer to a container and freeze.

Serve in chilled glasses with a mixture of fresh berries.

※ If you don't have an ice-cream maker, pour into a small baking tray and freeze, stir with a fork every few hours until amost frozen solid.

Valencia Cake with Orange Glaze

Serves 8

1 cup (250 ml/8½ fl oz) freshly
squeezed orange juice

2 teaspoons grated orange zest

a few threads of saffron,
crumbled

2 cups (300 g/10½ oz) plain
flour

pinch of salt

1½ teaspoons baking powder

1 cup (220 g/8 oz) caster sugar

1 whole egg and 1 egg white

¼ cup (60 g/2 oz) extra plain
yoghurt

3 tablespoons (60 ml/2 fl oz)
olive oil

GLAZE

1 tablespoon (20 ml/¾ fl oz)
orange marmalade

2 teaspoons orange liqueur,
such as Cointreau or Grand
Marnier

Preheat oven to 180°C (360°F). Lightly grease a 23-cm (10-in) cake tin and line base with baking paper.

Warm the orange juice, add orange zest and saffron, and leave to soak for 10 minutes. Meanwhile, sift the flour with the salt and baking powder into a small bowl.

Put sugar, whole egg and the egg white in a mixing bowl and beat at medium speed until thick and pale. Add yoghurt and beat to combine. Add oil and saffron-infused orange juice and beat again. Gradually fold in sifted flour until mixed.

Spoon batter into prepared cake tin. Bake in preheated oven for 40 minutes, or until a skewer inserted in centre comes out clean. Cake should be lightly browned and just coming away from the sides.

Leave to stand for 10 minutes, then invert on a cake cooler. When cool, place on serving platter.

To make glaze, put marmalade and liqueur in a small saucepan over medium heat. Simmer, stirring, until melted together. Strain over cake, and serve.

Almond Meringues

Soplillos

Makes about 30–36

150 g (5 oz) flaked almonds,
lightly toasted and finely
chopped

3 egg whites

pinch of salt

200 g (7 oz) caster sugar

1 teaspoon freshly squeezed
lemon juice

1–2 drops vanilla extract

2 teaspoons finely grated
lemon zest

whipped cream,
to serve (optional)

Preheat oven to 125°C (255°F). Line a mini-muffin pan with paper cases.

Put egg whites in a clean, dry bowl with the salt, and whisk until stiff. Add caster sugar gradually, a spoonful at a time, beating after each addition. When mixture is thick and glossy, beat in lemon juice and vanilla extract. Then carefully fold in the lemon zest and almonds.

Spoon mixture into the muffin cases. Place in preheated oven and bake for 30 minutes, then turn off oven and leave meringues to dry out (1–2 hours). If the meringues start to brown, cover with a sheet of baking paper.

Serve plain or with whipped cream.

※ If you prefer, you can make the meringues without paper cases and simply spoon the mixture into small piles on baking paper.

St James Cake

Torta de Santiago

Serves 8

150 g (4½ oz) plain flour, sifted

2 tablespoons (30 g/1 oz) caster sugar

½ teaspoon ground cinnamon

100 g (3½ oz) cold butter, chopped

1 egg yolk, lightly beaten

FILLING

3 eggs

100 g (3½ oz) caster sugar

200 g (8 oz) finely ground almonds

2 tablespoons finely grated lemon zest

2 tablespoons (40 ml/1½ fl oz) sweet sherry

icing sugar, for dusting

Preheat oven to 200°C (390°F). Lightly grease a 22-cm (8-in) non-stick tart dish with removable base.

To make the base, put flour, sugar, cinnamon, butter and egg yolk in a food processor and process till the mixture forms a dough. Roll dough into a ball, cover and refrigerate for 30 minutes.

Roll out dough on a lightly floured surface and use to line tart dish. Press into place, trim edges and prick base with a fork.

To make filling, whip eggs and sugar until frothy, then fold in almonds, lemon zest and sherry. Pour into tart shell and smooth the surface. **>**

Place tart in preheated oven and bake for 50 minutes. Remove from oven and leave in dish to cool.

When cold, transfer tart to a serving dish and dust top with icing sugar.

※ There are many variations of this cake, some with a pastry base and some without, but all have almonds and the tang of lemons.

※ The northern Spanish custom is to dust the icing sugar around a stencil shape of the cross of the Order of Santiago.

Little Doughnut Rings

Rosquillos

Serves 4

3 cups (450 g/1 lb) plain flour

1 teaspoon baking powder

200 ml (7 fl oz) milk

1 egg, beaten

100 ml (3½ fl oz) olive oil

1 teaspoon finely grated lemon zest

¼ teaspoon ground cinnamon

olive or vegetable oil for frying

½ teaspoon extra ground cinnamon mixed with caster sugar, to serve

Sift flour and baking powder into a large bowl.

Mix milk, egg, oil, lemon zest and cinnamon in a second bowl and stir well. Add to flour and mix until a soft dough forms (add a little extra flour if it seems too moist). Knead mixture for about 1 minute, then roll out on a lightly floured surface, to form ropes about 1.5 cm (⅝ in) thick and 15 cm (6 in) long. Join ends to form a ring or doughnut shape.

Heat oil in a heavy-based frying pan or deep-fryer until hot (180°C/360°F). Add dough rings a few at a time, and cook for 3–4 minutes, turning once, until golden. Drain on paper towel. Leave to cool, then dip into the caster sugar and cinnamon mix.

Custard Cream

Natillas

Serves 4

4 eggs

1 litre (34 fl oz) full-cream milk

¾ cup (150 g/5 oz) caster sugar

3 teaspoons cornflour

finely grated zest of 1 lemon

1 cinnamon stick

ground cinnamon, for dusting (optional)

Beat eggs with 1 cup (250 ml/8½ fl oz) of the milk, and the sugar and cornflour, until frothy.

Put remaining milk in a heavy-based saucepan with lemon zest and cinnamon stick, and bring just to the boil. Remove from heat, and discard cinnamon stick.

Put saucepan back over a low heat and gradually add egg mixture, stirring all the time, until the custard thickens (about 10 minutes).

Allow custard to cool a little, then pour into a large serving bowl or individual small bowls. Chill for a few hours or overnight.

Dust lightly with ground cinnamon, if desired, before serving.

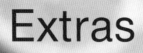

Extras

In many cases, a generous drizzle of Spain's renowned olive oil is all the sauce that accompanies a dish. But there are a few classic sauces that you might like to include in your repertoire.

It is definitely worth mastering *alioli*, a garlic-drenched mayonnaise especially typical of the Catalan region. It is often scooped onto fried potatoes, or used to add peppery creaminess to a fish stew or paella.

Capsicums and other peppers – and olives, of course – also feature in a range of traditional accompaniments, such as the smoky, piquant romesco sauce.

‹ Alioli (page 238)

Alioli

Makes 1½ cups

3 cloves garlic, crushed

2 teaspoons salt flakes

2 egg yolks, lightly beaten

1 cup (250 ml/8½ fl oz) extra-virgin olive oil

1 tablespoon (20 ml/¾ fl oz) freshly squeezed lemon juice

Pound garlic and salt in a mortar until you have a thick paste. Add egg yolks and mix until combined.

Pour garlic, salt and egg mixture into a food processor or blender. With the processor on, add the oil in a thin, slow, steady stream until you have a very thick mayonnaise. Stir in lemon juice. Adjust seasoning.

Keep, covered, in the fridge, until serving, to allow the flavours to develop.

※ A traditional alioli includes no eggs, only garlic and oil, but can be a little too potent for many tastes. A pinch of Spanish paprika can also be added. If short of time, use a good-quality egg mayonnaise and stir through some crushed garlic.

Green Sauce

Mojo verde

Makes 1¼ cups

¾ cup (185 ml/6½ fl oz) extra-virgin olive oil

3 green habanero chillies, deseeded and finely chopped

2 cloves garlic, chopped

1 spring onion, finely chopped

1 tablespoon finely chopped fresh coriander

1 teaspoon ground cumin

1 tablespoon (20 ml/¾ fl oz) white-wine vinegar

salt and freshly ground black pepper

Put all the ingredients in a food processor and pulse to a thick paste. Alternatively, you can pound everything, except the oil, in a mortar. When you have a thick paste, slowly add the oil to make a sauce.

Cover and refrigerate until needed. Serve with grilled fish, seafood or chicken.

Romesco Sauce

Makes about 2 cups

100 g (4 oz) raw almonds

100 g (4 oz) raw hazelnuts

2 large red capsicums, deseeded and thickly sliced

⅓ cup (80 ml/3 fl oz) olive oil

4 cloves garlic, sliced

2 slices stale white bread (crusts removed), cut into cubes

2 medium-sized, vine-ripened tomatoes, peeled and chopped

1 teaspoon ground sweet Spanish paprika

2 tablespoons (40 ml/1½ fl oz) red-wine vinegar

salt and freshly ground black pepper

Preheat oven to 180°C (360°F).

Put almonds and hazelnuts on a baking tray, place in preheated oven and cook for 5–10 minutes until they are lightly toasted and fragrant. Allow to cool, then rub to remove the skins. Roughly chop the nuts.

Put capsicum slices on a baking tray, drizzle with 1 tablespoon (20 ml/¾ fl oz) of the oil and roast for 15–20 minutes, or until softened. Leave to cool.

Heat oil in a non-stick frying pan over medium heat until hot. Add garlic and sauté for 1–2 minutes. Add bread cubes and cook for another minute or so, until lightly browned. Remove to a plate to cool.

Add tomatoes to the pan and cook for 5 minutes until softened.

Put roasted capsicum, garlic, fried bread, tomatoes, nuts, paprika and vinegar in a food processor and process until mixture is thick. Season with salt and pepper to taste. Store in refrigerator (for up to 2 days), but serve at room temperature.

✕ This piquant, bright-red sauce has innumerable variations and uses. It is delicious served as a dip with crusty bread, or a sauce for seafood or vegetables. You can thin it with a little water if needed.

Spanish Tapenade

Makes 1¾ cups

1½ cups pitted black Spanish olives

8–10 anchovy fillets in oil, drained

2 tablespoons capers, rinsed

½ cup (125 ml/4 fl oz) extra-virgin olive oil

finely grated zest of 1 lemon

sprig of fresh thyme

freshly ground black pepper

Place all the ingredients in a blender or food processor and pulse until mixed but still with some texture. Check for seasoning and add extra pepper if needed, and extra oil if mixture is a little dry.

Store, covered, in refrigerator, but serve at room temperature. Try it piled on slices of toasted breadstick as a quick, flavoursome tapa.

✕ This chunky paste is a Mediterranean favourite. It can be served (as above) as a tapa, with grilled chicken or fish, or as a dip with spring or summer vegetables.

Roasted Red Capsicum

Serves 4–6

4 red capsicums,
    deseeded and quartered

3 tablespoons (60 ml/2 fl oz)
    olive oil

1 tablespoon (20 ml/¾ fl oz)
    red-wine vinegar

1 clove garlic, crushed

1 spring onion, finely sliced

1 tablespoon chopped flat-leaf
    parsley

pinch sweet Spanish paprika

salt and freshly ground black
    pepper

Preheat oven to 200°C (390°F).

Place capsicum on a baking tray, drizzle with a little of the oil and roast in preheated oven for about 20 minutes, until softened and just starting to blacken around the edges. (Alternatively, you can grill or barbecue the capsicum.)

Place cooked capsicum in a bowl and cover with cling wrap to cool. When cool, peel off the skin, slice into strips and set aside.

Mix remaining olive oil with the vinegar, garlic, onion, parsley and paprika, and season with salt and pepper. Pour this marinade over the roasted capsicum, stir to coat and leave for at least a few hours for flavours to develop. (They will keep, covered in the fridge, for several days.) >

Bring the roasted capsicum to room temperature before serving – they are excellent served on a crusty tostado, but also go well with fish, grilled or barbecued meats, and in paellas and tortillas.

✕ You can buy roasted capsicum (loose, or in jars) from good delis and most supermarkets, but they are easy to prepare at home, and the flavour is worth it.

Sherry Vinaigrette

Makes 1 cup

¼ cup (60 ml/2 fl oz) sherry
  vinegar

¾ cup (185 ml/6½ fl oz) extra-
  virgin olive oil

1 clove garlic, crushed

½ teaspoon salt

Whisk together the vinegar, olive oil and garlic until combined. Season with a little salt.

Store, covered, in refrigerator, but allow to return to room temperature before using.

Special Ingredients

CAVA Spanish sparkling wine, made by the traditional Champagne method. The generic term *cava* (cave) reflects the original tradition of ageing the wine in underground cellars. Brut (dry) cava is recommended; if you can't find it, use any dry sparkling wine.

CHORIZO A pork sausage which gets its distinctive red colour from *pimenton* (Spanish paprika). There are numerous regional varieties of chorizo – smoked or unsmoked, mild or hot, with or without garlic and spices. Chorizo is available both cured (ready to eat) and fresh (which must be cooked before eating).

JAMON Cured ham; a Spanish specialty of which there are many regional variations. The best-known and most readily available is the dry-cured jamon serrano. The most highly-prized variety (and also the most expensive) is jamon Iberico, made from the flesh of acorn-fed, black Iberian pigs. If you are unable to buy jamon, you could substitute prosciutto.

MANCHEGO A semi-firm Spanish cheese made from sheep's milk. If it is not available you could use gruyere or a Swiss cheese.

PAELLA RICE For the very best results use a classic Spanish short-grain variety as grown in Calasparra. Bomba rice is the finest of these, as it can absorb three times its volume in liquid whilst still retaining its shape. If you cannot buy Spanish rice, arborio is an acceptable substitute.

PIMIENTO In Spanish, 'pimiento' refers to all sweet peppers of the capsicum family. Ranging from small to large, completely mild to extremely hot, pimientos come in red, green and yellow, and are an essential ingredient in much of Spanish cooking. Varieties popular in Spain include:

> **PADRON** Small, green, and sweetish; these peppers are mainly mild but notoriously, about one in ten is extremely hot!

> **PIQUILLO** Small red peppers which are charred over coals, peeled, and bottled or canned with olive oil and herbs. Available at specialist food outlets, Spanish delicatessens and some supermarkets.

RIOJA Wine from La Rioja province in Spain. Rioja is aged in oak barrels and can be red (*tinto*), white (*blanco*) or rosé (*rosado*).

SHERRY (*vino de Jerez*) A fortified wine made from white grapes grown near the Jerez region in Spain. Sherry is made in a variety of styles, from the light dry wines known as *fino*, to the rich, sweet dessert wines such as Pedro Ximenez.

SPANISH PAPRIKA (*pimenton*) An essential ingredient in Spanish cuisine, adding colour, spice and pungency, it is made from ripe, red pimientos that have been, dried, smoked and ground, and has a distinctive, strong smoky taste. Spanish paprika is available in sweet (*dulce*), mild (*agridulce*) and hot (*picante*) varieties.

VALDEON A rich, creamy Spanish blue cheese. Similar to roquefort.

Conversions

Important note: All cup and spoon measures given in this book are based on Australian standards. The most important thing to remember is that an Australian cup = 250 ml, while an American cup = 237 ml and a British cup = 284 ml. Also, an Australian tablespoon is equivalent to 4 teaspoons, not 3 teaspoons as in the United States and Britain. US equivalents have been provided throughout for all liquid cup/spoon measures. Equivalents for dry ingredients measured in cups/spoons have been included for flour, sugar and rising agents such as baking powder. For other dry ingredients (chopped vegetables, nuts, etc.), American cooks should be generous with their cup measures – slight variations in quantities of such ingredients are unlikely to affect results.

VOLUME

Australian cups/spoons	Millilitres	US fluid ounces
*1 teaspoon	5 ml	
1 tablespoon (4 teaspoons)	20 ml	¾ fl oz
1½ tablespoons	30 ml	1 fl oz
2 tablespoons	40 ml	1½ fl oz
¼ cup	60 ml	2 fl oz
⅓ cup	80 ml	3 fl oz
½ cup	125 ml	4 fl oz
¾ cup	180 ml	6 fl oz
1 cup	250 ml	8½ fl oz
4 cups	1 L	34 fl oz

*the volume of a teaspoon is the same around the world

SIZE

Centimetres	Inches
1 cm	⅜ in
2 cm	¾ in
2.5 cm	1 in
5 cm	2 in
10 cm	4 in
15 cm	6 in
20 cm	8 in
30 cm	12 in

TEMPERATURE

Celsius	Fahrenheit
150°C	300°F
160°C	320°F
170°C	340°F
180°C	360°F
190°C	375°F
200°C	390°F
210°C	410°F
220°C	420°F

WEIGHT

Grams	Ounces
15 g	½ oz
30 g	1 oz
60 g	2 oz
85 g	3 oz
110 g	4 oz
140 g	5 oz
170 g	6 oz
200 g	7 oz
225 g	8 oz (½ lb)
450 g	16 oz (1 lb)
500 g	1 lb 2 oz
900 g	2 lb
1 kg	2 lb 3 oz

Index

Alioli 237, 238
Alioli, Saffron 93
almonds
  Almond Biscuits (Polvorones) 222
  Almond & Chocolate Figs 195
  Almond Gazpacho (Ajo Blanco) 62
  Almond Lemon Cake 198
  Almond Meringues (Soplillos) 228
  Chickpeas with Tomatoes,
    Spinach & Almonds 171
  Garlic & Almond Picada 126
  Green Beans with Almonds & Cumin 143
  Greens, Valdeon Cheese
    & Smoked Almonds 131
  Monkfish with Saffron & Almonds 104
  Paprika-spiced Almonds 45
anchovies 3–4
  Anchovy & Egg Toast (Tostados) 13
  Anchovy & Olive Sticks (Gildas) 54
  Olive, Anchovy & Caper Puffs 59
  Piquillos with Anchovies 46
  Spanish Tapenade 242
  White Anchovy, Fennel & Lemon Salad
    (Ensalada de Boquerones) 135
Artichoke & Jamon Empanadas 12
asparagus
  Asparagus & Orange Salad 136
  Asparagus with Scrambled Eggs 14
  Jamon Iberico with Asparagus 36
Avocado Salsa 86

Baby Clams with Chorizo 105
Baby Leek Salad 125
Baby Squid on the Grill
  (Calamares a la Plancha) 91
Baked Garlic Mushroom Caps 18
Baked Sardines 107
Basque Fish Stew (Marmitako) 82

Basque-style Eggs (Piperada) 124
beans
  Broad Beans with Jamon 17
  Fava Bean Omelette 31
  Green Beans with Almonds & Cumin 143
  White Bean & Sausage Stew
    (Fabada Asturiana) 76
beetroot
  Slow-roasted Baby Beets with
    Goat's Curd & Hazelnuts 139
biscuits
  Almond Biscuits (Polvorones) 222
black pudding (morcilla) 4–5
  Fried Black Pudding (Morcilla Frita) 41
bread
  Catalan Bread with Tomato
    (Pa amd Tomaquet) 35
  croutons 63, 66
  see also toasts
Broad Beans with Jamon 17

cabbage
  Castilian Red Cabbage 144
cakes
  Almond Lemon Cake 198
  St James Cake (Torta de Santiago) 231
  Spanish Cakes (Magdalenas) 210
  Valencia Cake with Orange Glaze 226
capers
  Olive, Anchovy & Caper Puffs 59
  Spanish Tapenade 242
capsicum
  Basque-style Eggs (Piperada) 124
  Chargrilled Catalan Salad
    (Escalivada) 142
  Paella with Red Capsicum 148
  Roasted Red Capsicum 245
  Romesco Sauce 240

Spicy Chickpeas with
  Roasted Capsicum 114
Castilian Red Cabbage 144
Catalan Bread with Tomato
  (Pa amd Tomaquet) 35
Catalan Cream (Crema Catalana) 204
Cauliflower with Garlic & Almond Picada 126
cazuelas 9
cheese 249
  Cheese & Fig Open Sandwich
    (Montaditos de Manchego) 58
  Fried Cheese (Queso Frito) 51
  Goat's Cheese Toasts 70
  Greens, Valdeon Cheese
    & Smoked Almonds 131
  Quince & Blue Cheese Montaditos 52
  Slow-roasted Baby Beets with
    Goat's Curd & Hazelnuts 139
chicken
  Chicken with Sherry & Garlic 176
  Madrid Hotpot (Cocido Madrileno) 172
  Paella with Chicken & Rabbit
    (Paella a la Valenciana) 150
  Saffron Chicken with Garlic Picada 188
  Sherry Chicken with Orange 186
chickpeas
  Chickpea & Cod Soup 64
  Chickpeas & Chorizo 26
  Chickpeas with Tomatoes,
    Spinach & Almonds 171
  Madrid Hotpot (Cocido Madrileno) 172
  Spicy Chickpeas with
    Roasted Capsicum 114
chocolate
  Almond & Chocolate Figs 195
  Chocolate Sauce 203
  Fig Roll (Pan de Higo) 213
Chorizo 248
  Baby Clams with Chorizo 105
  Chickpeas & Chorizo 26
  Chorizo Omelette (Tortilla al Chorizo) 158
  Chorizo in Red Wine 30
  White Bean & Sausage Stew
    (Fabada Asturiana) 76

clams
  Baby Clams with Chorizo 105
  Clams in Fresh Tomato Sauce 168
Coffee Liqueur Flan 207
conversions 250–1
croutons 63, 66
Crumbed Mussels 98
cucumber
  Gazpacho Andalucia 74
  Tomato & Cucumber Salad (Pipirrana) 132
custard
  Catalan Cream (Crema Catalana) 204
  Coffee Liqueur Flan 207
  Custard Cream (Natillas) 234
  Custard Tarts 217
  Fried Milk (Leche Frita) 215

doughnuts
  Little Doughnut Rings (Rosquillos) 233
  Spanish Doughnuts (Churros) 201

eggplants
  Chargrilled Catalan Salad
    (Escalivada) 142
eggs
  Anchovy & Egg Toast (Tostados) 13
  Asparagus with Scrambled Eggs 14
  Basque-style Eggs (Piperada) 124
  Eggs with Tuna (Huevos con Atun) 39
Empanadas
  Artichoke & Jamon Empanadas 12
  Empanadillas with Tuna 19
  Spinach Empanadas 55
equipment 9

Fava Bean Omelette 31
fennel
  White Anchovy, Fennel & Lemon Salad
    (Ensalada de Boquerones) 135
figs
  Almond & Chocolate Figs 195
  Cheese & Fig Open Sandwich
    (Montaditos de Manchego) 58
  Fig Roll (Pan de Higo) 213
  Figs with Oranges & Walnuts 197

fish
  Baked Sardines 107
  Basque Fish Stew (Marmitako) 82
  Galician Fish Soup 66
  Jamon-wrapped Fish 32
  Marinated Fish (Escabeche) 100
  Monkfish with Saffron & Almonds 104
  Sardines Chargrilled in Vine Leaves 94
  Trout with Jamon 106
  Whitebait with Saffron Alioli 93
  see also anchovies; salt cod; tuna
flans
  Coffee Liqueur Flan 207
Fried Black Pudding (Morcilla Frita) 42
Fried Cheese (Queso Frito) 51
Fried Milk (Leche Frita) 215
Fried Spanish Olives 57
Fried Squid (Calamares Fritos) 23

Galician Fish Soup 66
Galician-style Octopus (Pulpo Gallego) 92
garlic
  Alioli 237, 238
  Baked Garlic Mushroom Caps 18
  Chicken with Sherry & Garlic 176
  Garlic & Almond Picada 126
  Garlic & Chilli Mushrooms 29
  Garlic Picada 188
  Garlic Prawns (Gambas al Ajillo) 87
  Garlic Soup 69
  Saffron Alioli 93
Gazpacho Andalucía 74
Goat's Cheese Toasts 70
Golden Saffron Potatoes 130
Green Beans with Almonds & Cumin 143
Green Sauce (Mojo Verde) 239
Greens, Valdeon Cheese
  & Smoked Almonds 131
Gypsy Stew (Olla Gitana) 79

Ham Croquettes (Croquetas de Jamon) 37
hotpot
  Madrid Hotpot (Cocido Madrileno) 172

jamon 4, 249
  Artichoke & Jamon Empanadas 12
  Broad Beans with Jamon 17
  Ham Croquettes (Croquetas de Jamon) 37
  Jamon Iberico with Asparagus 36
  Jamon-wrapped Fish 32
  Pork Rolls with Jamon Serrano 48
  Trout with Jamon 106

Kidneys with Sherry (Rinones al Jerez) 40

lamb
  Slow-cooked Lamb with Lemon 190
leeks
  Baby Leek Salad 125
  Lentils with Mushrooms & Leeks 121
lemon
  Almond Lemon Cake 198
  Slow-cooked Lamb with Lemon 190
  White Anchovy, Fennel & Lemon Salad
    (Ensalada de Boquerones) 135
Lentil & Pork Soup 73
Lentils with Mushrooms & Leeks 121
Little Doughnut Rings (Rosquillos) 233

Madrid Hotpot (Cocido Madrileno) 172
Marinated Fish (Escabeche) 100
mayonnaise see alioli
meatballs
  Spanish Meatballs (Albondigas) 161
meringues
  Almond Meringues (Soplillos) 228
Monkfish with Saffron & Almonds 104
mushrooms
  Baked Garlic Mushroom Caps 18
  Garlic & Chilli Mushrooms 29
  Lentils with Mushrooms & Leeks 121
mussels
  Crumbed Mussels 98
  debearding 7
  Mussels in White Wine 88

nuts see almonds; walnuts

octopus
    Galician-style Octopus (Pulpo Gallego) 92
    preparing 7–8
olive oil 5–6
olives
    Anchovy & Olive Sticks (Gildas) 54
    Fried Spanish Olives 57
    Olive, Anchovy & Caper Puffs 59
    Spanish Tapenade 242
    Spiced Olives 53
    Spinach with Olives & Pine Nuts 129
omelettes
    Chorizo Omelette (Tortilla al Chorizo) 158
    Fava Bean Omelette 31
    Spanish Omelette (Tortilla Espagnola) 156
Onion & Orange Salad 141
oranges
    Asparagus & Orange Salad 136
    Figs with Oranges & Walnuts 197
    Onion & Orange Salad 141
    Seville Oranges with
      Cinnamon Wine Syrup 209
    Sherry Chicken with Orange 186
    Valencia Cake with Orange Glaze 226
Oxtail Braised in Red Wine 181

Padron Peppers 41, 248
paella 147
    Paella with Chicken & Rabbit
      (Paella a la Valenciana) 150
    Paella with Red Capsicum 148
    rice for 149, 249
    Seafood Paella (Paella a la Marinera) 153
    paella pan 9
paprika (Spanish) 6, 249
    Paprika Prawns with Avocado Salsa 86
    Paprika-spiced Almonds 45
pastries
    Custard Tarts 217
    Olive, Anchovy & Caper Puffs 59
    Walnut Pastry Puffs (Casadielles) 194
    see also empanadas
Peaches Poached in Red Wine 220
peppers see padron; piquillo

picada
    Garlic & Almond Picada 126
    Garlic Picada 188
piquillo peppers 248
    Piquillos with Anchovies 46
pork
    Lentil & Pork Soup 73
    Pork Belly with Thyme & Red Wine 183
    Pork Rolls with Jamon Serrano 48
    Pork Skewers (Pinchitos) 47
    Roast Pork Loin with Pedro Ximenez 163
    Spanish Meatballs (Albondigas) 161

potatoes
    Golden Saffron Potatoes 130
    Potatoes with Garlic Mayo
      (Patatas Alioli) 115
    Salt Cod Baked with Potatoes 165
    Salt Cod Fritters (Bunuelos de Bacalao) 24
    Spanish Omelette (Tortilla Espagnola) 156
    Spicy Potatoes (Patatas Bravas) 116
prawns
    Garlic Prawns (Gambas al Ajillo) 87
    Paprika Prawns with Avocado Salsa 86
    Prawn Fritters 97
    preparing 8

Quail Roasted in Vine Leaves 179
Quince & Blue Cheese Montaditos 52

rabbit
    Paella with Chicken & Rabbit
      (Paella a la Valenciana) 150
    Rabbit with Pancetta & Thyme 174
    Rabbit & Tomato Stew 81
Raspberry & Cava Sorbet 225
rice
    for paella 149, 249
    Rice Pudding (Arroz con leche) 196
Roast Pork Loin with Pedro Ximenez 163
Roasted Red Capsicum 245
Romesco Sauce 240
Russian Salad (Ensaladilla Rusa) 123
Rustic Squid Stew 75

saffron 6–7
  Golden Saffron Potatoes 130
  Monkfish with Saffron & Almonds 104
  Saffron Alioli 93
  Saffron Chicken with Garlic Picada 188
  St James Cake (Torta de Santiago) 231
salads
  Asparagus & Orange Salad 136
  Baby Leek Salad 125
  Chargrilled Catalan Salad (Escalivada) 142
  Greens, Valdeon Cheese
    & Smoked Almonds 131
  Onion & Orange Salad 141
  Russian Salad (Ensaladilla Rusa) 123
  Tomato & Cucumber Salad (Pipirrana) 132
  White Anchovy, Fennel & Lemon Salad
    (Ensalada de Boquerones) 135
salsa
  Avocado Salsa 86
salt cod (bacalao) 4
  Chickpea & Cod Soup 64
  preparing 4
  Salt Cod Baked with Potatoes 165
  Salt Cod Fritters (Bunuelos de Bacalao) 24
  Salt Cod Pureé (Brandada de bacalao) 20
sardines
  Baked Sardines 107
  Sardines Chargrilled in Vine Leaves 94
sauces
  Chocolate Sauce 203
  Fresh Tomato Sauce 168
  Green Sauce (Mojo Verde) 239
  Red-wine Sauce 183
  Romesco Sauce 240
  see also Alioli
Scallops in White Wine 109
seafood 85
  Galician-style Octopus (Pulpo Gallego) 92
  Scallops in White Wine 109
  Seafood Paella (Paella a la Marinera) 153
  see also clams; fish; mussels; prawns;
    squid
Seville Oranges with
  Cinnamon Wine Syrup 209

Sherry (Vino de Jerez) 5, 249
  Chicken with Sherry & Garlic 176
  Kidneys with Sherry (Rinones al Jerez) 40
  Pedro Ximenez 5
  Roast Pork Loin with Pedro Ximenez 163
  Sherry Chicken with Orange 186
  Sherry Vinaigrette 247
  sherry vinegar 7
Slow-cooked Lamb with Lemon 190
Slow-roasted Baby Beets with
  Goat's Curd & Hazelnuts 139
sorbet
  Raspberry & Cava Sorbet 225
soup 61
  Almond Gazpacho (Ajo blanco) 62
  Chickpea & Cod Soup 64
  Galician Fish Soup 66
  Garlic Soup 69
  Gazpacho Andalucía 74
  Lentil & Pork Soup 73
  Spanish Tomato Soup with
    Goat's Cheese Toasts 70
Spanish Cakes (Magdalenas) 210
Spanish Doughnuts (Churros) 201
Spanish Meatballs (Albondigas) 161
Spanish Omelette (Tortilla Espagnola) 156
Spanish Tapenade 242
Spanish Tomato Soup with
  Goat's Cheese Toasts 70
Spiced Olives 53
Spicy Chickpeas with Roasted Capsicum 114
Spicy Potatoes (Patatas Bravas) 116
spinach 8–9
  Chickpeas with Tomatoes,
    Spinach & Almonds 171
  Spinach Empanadas 55
  Spinach with Olives & Pine Nuts 129
squid
  Baby Squid on the Grill
    (Calamares a la Plancha) 91
  Fried Squid (Calamares Fritos) 23
  preparing 8–9
  Rustic Squid Stew 75
  Squid with Peas 110

stews
  Basque Fish Stew (Marmitako) 82
  Gypsy Stew (Olla Gitana) 79
  Rabbit & Tomato Stew 81
  Rustic Squid Stew 75
  White Bean & Sausage Stew
    (Fabada Asturiana) 76
Stuffed Tomatoes (Tomatoes rellenos) 118

tapas 11
  recipes 12–59
tapenade
  Spanish Tapenade 242
tarts
  Custard Tarts 217
toasts (tostados)
  Anchovy & Egg Toast (Tostados) 13
  Cheese & Fig Open Sandwich
    (Montaditos de Manchego) 58
  Goat's Cheese Toasts 70
  Tuna Toasts (Tostados de Atun) 102
tomatoes
  Basque-style Eggs (Piperada) 124
  Catalan Bread with Tomato
    (Pa amd Tomaquet) 35
  Chargrilled Catalan Salad (Escalivada) 142
  Chickpeas with Tomatoes,
    Spinach & Almonds 171
  Gazpacho Andalucía 74
  Rabbit & Tomato Stew 81
  Spanish Tomato Soup with
    Goat's Cheese Toasts 70
  Stuffed Tomatoes (Tomatoes Rellenos) 118
  Tomato & Cucumber Salad
    (Pipirrana) 132

Trout with Jamon 106
tuna
  Eggs with Tuna (Huevos con Atun) 39
  Empanadillas with Tuna 19
  Marinated Fish (Escabeche) 100
  Tuna Toasts (Tostados de Atun) 102

Valencia Cake with Orange Glaze 226
vinaigrette
  Sherry Vinaigrette 247
vine leaves
  Quail Roasted in Vine Leaves 179
  Sardines Chargrilled in Vine Leaves 94

walnuts
  Figs with Oranges & Walnuts 197
  Walnut Pastry Puffs (Casadielles) 194
White Anchovy, Fennel & Lemon Salad
  (Ensalada de Boquerones) 135
White Bean & Sausage Stew
  (Fabada Asturiana) 76
Whitebait with Saffron Aioli 93
wine 5, 248, 249
  Chorizo in Red Wine 30
  Cinnamon Wine Syrup 209
  Mussels in White Wine 88
  Oxtail Braised in Red Wine 181
  Peaches Poached in Red Wine 220
  Pork Belly with Thyme & Red Wine 183
  Raspberry & Cava Sorbet 225
  Scallops in White Wine 109
  see also sherry

LONDON, NEW YORK, MUNICH,
MELBOURNE AND DELHI

First published in Great Britain in 2011 by
Dorling Kindersley, 80 Strand, London, WC2R 0RL

A Penguin Company

Published by Penguin Group (Australia), 2010
250 Camberwell Road, Camberwell, Victoria 3124, Australia
(a division of Pearson Australia Group Pty Ltd)

10 9 8 7 6 5 4 3 2 1

Text and photographs copyright © Penguin Group (Australia), 2010

The moral right of the author has been asserted.

Design by Marley Flory & Nikki Townsend © Penguin Group (Australia)
Photography by Julie Renouf
Food styling by Lee Blaylock
Typeset in Nimbus Sans Novus by Post Pre-press Group, Brisbane, Queensland
Scanning and separations by Splitting Image P/L, Clayton, Victoria
Printed and bound in China by Everbest Printing Co. Ltd

A CIP catalogue record for this book is available from the British Library.

ISBN: 978-1-4053-6416-4

Discover more at www.dk.com